PREFACE TO
THE STUDY OF PAUL

Preface to
the Study of Paul

STEPHEN WESTERHOLM

WILLIAM B. EERDMANS PUBLISHING COMPANY
GRAND RAPIDS, MICHIGAN / CAMBRIDGE, U.K.

© 1997 Wm. B. Eerdmans Publishing Co.
255 Jefferson Ave. S.E., Grand Rapids, Michigan 49503 /
P.O. Box 163, Cambridge CB3 9PU U.K.

Printed in the United States of America

01 00 99 98 97   7 6 5 4 3 2 1

Library of Congress Cataloging-in-Publication Data

Westerholm, Stephen, 1949-
    Preface to the study of Paul / Stephen Westerholm.
        p.   cm.
    ISBN 0-8028-4258-5
    1. Bible. N.T. Epistles of Paul — Study and teaching. 2. Bible.
N.T. Romans — Criticism, interpretation, etc. 3. Paul, the Apostle,
Saint.   I. Title.
    BS2650.5.W47   1997
    227'.06 — dc21
                                                    96-49741
                                                        CIP

With love, to
  Jessica, Martin, Paul, and Monica
    — each a gift of Love

Contents

Introduction

TWO THOUSAND years later, Paul attracts more attention than any other figure from antiquity but one. Within the academy, anthropological readings of the apostle are heaped upon feminist which are heaped upon historical which are heaped upon liberationist or Marxist which are heaped upon psychological which are heaped upon rhetorical which are heaped upon sociological which are heaped upon theological. One is loathe to interrupt such industry. But one can well imagine an outsider — a Herbert, if you will — wanting to pose what to him seems an obvious question: Why *Paul?*

With all due respect, Herbert doubts that Paul's significance can lie in his peculiar suitability for anthropological, psychological, or sociological study. Ancient rhetoric, Herbert confesses, is not, for him, a long-standing interest; but if it were, there are authors he would read before Paul. On the surface, then, the preoccupations of the Pauline industry provide no explanation for its existence. Herbert has, to be sure, his own hunch about what has happened: Paul, important on other grounds, has attracted much — and diverse — scholarly attention. Outsider that he is, Herbert wonders what those "other grounds" might be. Until he has grasped them and can decide for himself whether they hold any interest, Herbert will tip his hat to the industry — and go his separate way.

Before a client is allowed to escape, however, the industry makes its time-honored pitch: Paul (Herbert is assured) did more than any other for the early spread of Christianity; letters in his name comprise half the books of the New Testament; his epistle to the Romans is, by a wide margin, the most influential nonnarrative account of the Christian faith ever written; its impact on such giants of Western religiosity as Augustine, Luther, Wesley, and Barth has been profound. . . . The litany could continue, but Herbert will have long since broken it off. Everyone *knows* (vaguely, to be sure, but sufficiently to satisfy themselves on this count) that Paul looms large in the pages of history. The issue remains *why*. What (as Herbert himself would put it) is "so big about Paul"? What have people seen in him? Why did *he* make such an impact? Fair questions, all. To satisfy Herbert, we must dig a little deeper.

Even casual readers of his letters sense that Paul was a man completely captivated by a particular vision of reality; those who met him must have been similarly struck — and, for many, his captivation proved contagious. The vision Paul communicated both reoriented and gave significance to their lives; it provided them with a sense of what they should and should not do, and motivation for doing what (in the light of the vision) they were convinced was right and worthwhile. In the nearly two thousand years that have since passed, Paul's letters have played essentially the same role: they have proved, for millions of readers, a compelling, illuminating, and treasured guide to life.

The record, by any reckoning, is impressive. Few authors can match Paul's staying power; few, the breadth of his readership. Will Herbert be interested? If he is like most of his contemporaries, he has little practice in posing basic questions about life and less education that would encourage him to do so. Confront him with the dictum that "the unexamined life is not worth living," and Herbert's face will register an eloquent blankness: he has nary an inkling how one would "examine life" or assess the worth of its pursuits. Still, vigorously put, such issues will engage all but the most comatose of readers. And Paul puts them vigorously — none more so: therein, in a nutshell, lie his impact and appeal. Herbert, so informed, can decide for himself whether to take up the challenge or leave it.

Contemporary readers of Paul, however, soon encounter difficulties. The assumptions underlying Paul's vision are not shared by many moderns, and effort is needed if they are to become intelligible. Scholars themselves do not always face up to the dilemma. Whatever their intentions, they foster only the parochial arrogance of the modern West if they convey just enough of Paul's thinking (or that of any other ancient) to impress students with its "weirdness." The same result is achieved if they avoid the "weird" and focus only on aspects of Paul's thought related to current notions and concerns. Students, with their unchallenged modern perspective, then simply accept what suits their accustomed ways of thinking and reject the rest — hardly an educational experience! We have not understood Paul, nor can we judge him fairly, until we have grasped how what repels as well as what attracts us makes sense on *his* presuppositions. One need not, in the end, be convinced by Paul to comprehend him; one must, at the least, see how others could find him convincing. Like all genuine encounters with foreign cultures and ways of thinking, such a stretching of our mental horizons will alert us to presuppositions of our own that we otherwise take as axiomatic.

Modern students of Paul's letters need a preface to his thought that addresses the gaps between his horizons and their own. In what follows, I will allow the argument of Paul's letter to the Romans to determine both the issues raised and the sequence with which they are dealt. Such a procedure should offset somewhat the temptation to impose our own systems on Paul's thought or to deal only with aspects of Paul deemed relevant for a modern readership. Discussion (particularly in the early chapters) will focus less on what Paul says than on the assumptions that underlie it. Topics treated in standard introductions to Romans will here be ignored: the dating of the epistle, the beginnings of Christianity in Rome, the character of the Roman Christian community, and the like. Not only is such material readily available elsewhere; until moderns themselves find Paul engaging, such questions are only of academic interest (that is, they are thought worth pursuing only by students assured that "they will be on the exam"). Rather, the immediate task is to engage. Nor should anyone confuse what follows with a commentary on the details of the epistle. The goal here is to make comprehensible the major components of Paul's vision of life as they are raised in his most important letter.

I should perhaps say (the industry will expect it) that the letter to the Romans *is* a letter, addressed to a particular community at a particular time; in short, hardly the sort of document in which one would expect to find any very systematic statement of Paul's convictions. Some industry spokespeople would want me to add that Paul did not think very systematically; a few, indeed, think him so incoherent that any project such as mine is misguided. If I must justify proceeding with it, I would say that (1) Romans is a *more* systematic statement of fundamental Pauline convictions than is any other extant letter (presumably because Paul was introducing himself to a community most of whom knew him only by hearsay); furthermore, (2) while none of us is as coherent as we like to think, Paul, I persist in believing, was more so than some of his recent detractors have allowed. That is a thesis, of course, requiring demonstration. What should be apparent to all is that the Paul of Romans attempts to place specific issues in a broad context, that he feels the need to relate his convictions to each other, draw out their implications, and answer questions that arise from them. In any case, (3) whether or not *we* find Paul's thinking systematic or even coherent, a substantial number of people over a significant period of time have found it compelling. It must be legitimate to ask why.

And so we turn to the thought-world of Paul. Surrounded by mega-malls, by multilayered highways and multicolored smog, we find it easy to forget that the world of our disguises was once the world of the apostle. So novel are contemporary expressions of the human quest for knowledge, power, gratification, and love that we are tempted to overlook the generic likeness between our lives, still spanning threescore years and ten, and his. Yet apologists of the modern age who see history as a one-way street of unimpeded progress are fewer today than they were scant decades ago. Realistic scorecards pitting the contemporary scene against that of bygone eras now show losses as well as gains; and so they must, if we are not to forget entire dimensions of the human experience. But to keep an honest score, the past must be studied for other purposes than to satisfy antiquarian curiosity or to fuel the indignation of modern ideologies. More demanding of patience and imagination is the task of reconstructing the world as it once appeared, and made sense, to our fellow human beings; yet academics fail their generation if they do not transmit such alternative visions against which moderns may measure their own. Within the world as Paul described it, millions of people for nearly two millenia have lived and found meaningful the vicissitudes of their lives. It is a vision, one can only conclude, with sufficient cogency and depth to intrigue and challenge moderns as well — provided they are equipped to understand it.

Chapter 1

The Commission and Its Context

ROMANS 1:1-15

THE OPENING of Romans offers nothing to cheer those who would fain believe that even Paul must, on occasion, have engaged in small talk. He presents himself at the outset as a man under commission, briefly defines his assigned task, then declares that he has long desired to meet his readers in person — for the rather *im*personal reason that they, too, fall within the sphere of his mandate. A passage toward the end of the letter indicates that he undertook its writing (to discharge apostolic responsibilities among the Romans that circumstances had kept him from fulfilling by other means)[1] In short, the only Paul we encounter in Romans is one acting very consciously in what he regarded as his appointed office: that of an "apostle."

Our interest here is in seeing the world through Paul's (ever so apostolic) eyes: in grasping something of the way Paul came to view, and convinced others to view, the nature and terms of human existence. But in these opening verses, he provides only a brief summary of *what* it is that he communicates to others, using terms ("gospel of God," "son of God," "resurrection from the dead") that we may more conveniently explore when they become central to his argument. What dominates the introduction is not the substance of Paul's message but the claim that he has been commissioned to promote it. This sense of mission — the sense that he has been given a significant part to play in a drama that is nonetheless much bigger than he is — surfaces constantly in

1. See Romans 15:15-22.

Paul's writings. We do well to begin, as he begins Romans, with his apostolic self-understanding.

A Man under Commission

Unsympathetic readings of Paul are wont to characterize him as self-important, authoritarian, opinionated, and intolerant. Paul would have responded with an apostolic huff — and, from his perspective, not without reason. Self-important? What can we expect of a man convinced, first, that he lived at the turning-point in the conflict of the ages between good and evil, and, second, that, through a role-casting that surprised no one more than himself, he had been entrusted with the task of enlisting the non-Jews of the world on the side of the good? Not all will think the drama credible; none can fault one who found it so for playing his part to the hilt. Authoritarian? In all fairness, we should note that Paul was not as rigid on some issues as he was on most. Even in the latter cases, he justified his firmness, not with a simple insistence upon his prerogatives as an apostle, but with an appeal to considerations that he believed telling for his readers as well as for himself. Moreover, he exempted himself from no constraints or sacrifices that he imposed upon others. That being said, we may concede that Paul showed a singular aptitude for demanding compliance. Yet among the tasks that require such a facility, his own — as *he* understood it and the stakes it involved — must surely be reckoned preeminent. Opinionated? Intolerant? Again, such captions are flatly contradicted by *parts* of the evidence. And when Paul was as inflexible as only he could be, he would, in his own mind, have betrayed his commission had he acted differently. Nor, for that matter, would he have allowed that the subjects of his insistence were his own opinions. At issue, from his perspective, were truths that he had been obliged to accept in the light of his commissioning. Loyalty to an awesome task, for which he would be held awesomely responsible, required him to uphold them. He did so — one must concede — with admirable vigor.

The root of the problem that many moderns have with Paul is thus not our distaste for his self-importance, authoritarianism, or intolerance, but our (perhaps subconscious) penchant for discounting a claim to which we are not disposed to give credence: that Paul had been commissioned by the resurrected "son of God." The contemporary dismissal of this particular claim can be placed in a wider context: the worldview of many moderns will not admit of "revelation" from any "supernatural" source. Paul's convictions were not so constricted. If, then, we were to assume that what makes no sense on our own presuppositions cannot have been meant seriously by Paul, we would only be betraying our own cultural blinders. That he was indeed convinced that he had been commissioned by the resurrected Christ is apparent on several counts: from the redirection of his life that his conviction occasioned (the change from foe to champion of the Christian cause will not, in Paul's day, have been prompted by the prudence of the worldly wise); from the energy he devoted to the fulfillment of his perceived mandate; from the fervor of the religious convictions Paul held because he believed he had seen God's "son"; from his loyalty to both commission and convictions in the face of hardship and death. In his own mind, Paul was an authorized representative of Jesus Christ. And he applied himself to his august task with a passion and a single-mindedness so remarkable that his readers have been left in doubt whether the man was even pervious to the charms of small talk.

The Framework of the Commission

The problem remains: How are moderns to enter the thought-world of one convinced that he had experienced what their own horizons exclude as impossible? This difficulty will occupy us throughout the pages that follow. Still, an initial sketch of a pathway into Paul's world — to be filled in with more detail in subsequent chapters — may help us understand how Paul's commission would be seen from within his own horizons.

Newspapers commonly report that a happy, healthy, vivacious child was kidnapped, abused, murdered. We cannot but wonder, on reading such stories, what kind of world we inhabit. Of the many answers that could be given, I will briefly summarize two as a reminder that the same events are susceptible of different interpretations; a third perspective we will consider at somewhat greater length as our entrée to the thought-world of Paul.

1. The vibrant, innocent life of a child is rightly valued by humans; we deplore its brutal curtailment. Such incidents reveal the utter indifference of the universe to the values and sensibilities of human beings. The world continues on its chaotic way after, as before, a child's life is snuffed out. Apart from humans, "all that is" is only a purposeless conglomerate of matter. Value and meaning are exclusively the products of human intelligence, feeling, and will. Yet human possibilities of imposing order on "reality" are very limited. Inevitably, cold, indifferent nature wins in the end. We can only affirm — in no one's hearing but our own — that our efforts have made the interval worthwhile.

2. The child's life was good, its curtailment evil. Human history represents only one of the battlefields on which eternally opposed, superhuman forces wage their constant struggle: powers of creation and destruction, order and chaos, life and death, goodness and evil.

3. The life of a child is good, a precious gift and cause for celebration. So, each in its own right, is the life of the great horned owl, the bay-breasted wood warbler, the great northern pike, and the yellow damselfish. That there are harlequin tuskfish and shingle-back skinks is good, whether or not humans are aware of their existence. Indeed, *all* that is, because it is and because it has a part in "all that is," is good. Humans are themselves but a part of "all that is," distinctive as each species is distinct, but too obviously related to the rest of creation to imagine that they alone give it meaning or worth. Like many another species, they are born, then sustained in early life by those to whom they owe their birth; they grow in stature, and in knowledge as they do so; they learn to procure their livelihood; they love and are loved; they couple, reproduce, then care — at great sacrifice to themselves — for the new life with which they have been entrusted. We are but a part of this world. It is not of our design or making, nor are we the source of its goodness. For that we must look to the great Lover of life and beauty, who is eternal and good.

Yet children are murdered in this world. It does not follow that the cosmos is itself without value and indifferent to goodness; only that it has become the scene of much that is evil. The evil is real: neither good (like the life of a child) *nor* evil (like the murder of a child) exists only in human minds. Evil is that which resists and disrupts what is good. Yet evil is not, like good, eternal. By its very resistant, disruptive nature, evil is parasitic, depending on the prior existence of the good to which it inappropriately responds. We live neither in a world to which we alone bring value, nor in one in which good and evil are co-equal combatants. Our world is essentially and wonderfully good, but profoundly and horribly disturbed by things that ought never, and need never, have occurred.

All three interpretations (and others could, of course, be cited) provide a framework within which the murder of a child can be understood. They conflict and cannot all be true on any fundamental level (though they could, of course, all be false).[2] We may be inclined to conclude that, given the plethora of possible interpretations, our attempts to arrive at the truth of such matters are pointless: better to content ourselves with the demands and satisfactions of life immediately before us. But such is an impoverished human existence — and it is not academic arrogance that labels it so. The academic may lament that Kant, Kierkegaard, and Camus are too little read, believing that familiarity with their work can enrich our human experience. But we need not be academics to realize that, without *some* framework, *some* vision of what life is about, we have no explanation for why we do what we do; no resource for distinguishing worthwhile pursuits from trivial; no basis for answering the moral questions of a child; no language for articulating the significance of turning-points in our lives; no nonsedative means for coping with tragedy. None of us ever does live without *some* kind of interpretive framework. But we differ widely in the degree of thoughtfulness with which we live, the consistency with which we approach the various aspects of our lives, the coherence of the framework that — consciously or unconsciously — we find ourselves adopting.

Some framework is needed; at some levels, most any framework will serve. But human curiosity, our insatiable capacity to wonder and question, will demand at some point what truth there may be in the

---

2. The conceit that *no* human construction corresponds to reality represents a fashionably self-contradictory variant of the first interpretation: construing reality as chaotic, it declares that no construction of reality can be true. If, however, reality has meaningful order, as the sages of other ages have believed, then there is no antecedent reason why the human mind, itself a fragment of the whole, cannot capture a glimpse of the latter's awesome symmetry. On any reading, human perceptions never exhaust reality.

framework that we have adopted; whether our pursuits are worthwhile in any forum other than that of our own imaginings; whether we are answering or only pacifying the queries of a child. Such questions can hardly be posed of any framework until we have a fair grasp of the framework as a whole and of how things "look" from within its boundaries. Only then can we ask whether such a way of viewing life is coherent, whether it can do justice to all that we know of human experience, whether it gives value to what we sense must be valued, and so on. These latter are essential, human questions, but they lie beyond our purview here. Our more limited goal is the preliminary one of finding a basis for understanding a particular, widely influential, now widely forgotten, vision.

The Appropriateness of the Commission

Paul's vision of reality is, of course, a variant of the third interpretation sketched above. Such a summary provokes myriads of doubts and queries: How can evil originate in a world supposedly good? How can a God supposedly good permit it to happen? How does one explain the existence of natural (in addition to moral) evil? These questions all have their place. But our immediate concern in this chapter is how a commission such as Paul believed he had received, though incredible to many moderns, made sense to him.

If nonhuman reality is without inherent value, with only mechanical order, then Paul's "commission" as he understood it is impossible.[3] But things look very different to the Jewish or Christian mind. If "all that is," including the Source of "all that is," is — in its essence — good, then evil is both a disruption of "what is" and an affront to its Source. Yet the Source of "all that is" has surely the resources to deal with such an eventuality. Moreover, being by nature good, God will not be inclined

---

3. Indeed, if we are to maintain such an interpretive framework, we must refuse credence to any and every claim of religious experience. None can be accepted in its own terms; all must be given nonreligious explanations. Religious people themselves are wont to see here a weakness in a mechanical, "naturalistic" worldview.

to ignore the appearance and threat of evil. Divine intervention in a world gone awry is not only expected but demanded.

Furthermore, on this interpretation, nature's regularities are themselves the work of God and hardly to be interfered with by caprice; yet (still on this interpretation) that God should signal his interventions with striking *departures* from nature's norms (that is, with "miracles") cannot be thought strange. Paul, bound for Damascus, did not expect to meet the risen Christ. Still, he knew what to make of such a happening. It was certainly extraordinary — it would *have* to be extraordinary to get *his* attention — but hardly incredible. Incredible in Paul's eyes would have been rather the suggestion that the God of life and love would permit evil to encroach uninterrupted on the goodness of his creation: that was far more unbelievable than that the God who created life should restore it to the dead. To Paul's mind, then, the startling way in which he was charged with his mandate was only suited to its import: to proclaim God's stunning response to evil and the decisive triumph of the Good.

In the chapters that follow, we will attempt to retrieve the vision of life worked out by Paul in the light of what he believed to be a divine revelation and commissioning. One further aspect of the task itself warrants mention here. Paul's mission, as he saw it, was to the world's non-Jews (or "Gentiles"; in Paul's language, *ethnē*, "nations," "peoples"). The presumption that humanity can be meaningfully categorized as "Jews" and "all the rest" is itself telling of Paul's horizons. Note, further, the movement of truth *from* Jews *to* "all the rest": it pertains to Jews first in so real a sense that its spread to Gentiles puts the latter in the former's debt.[4] More is meant than that recent events of extraordinary significance have taken place among Jews. Rather, those events are seen as the climax of a whole series of divine interventions involving Jews: interventions to which Jews, moreover, have been given the interpretive key.[5] The intended beneficiaries include all nations and, ultimately, all creation;[6] but Jews are seen as the effective channels of divine benevolence. Much of the dynamics of Romans is provided by Paul's dual insistence on (1) the universal goal of the

---

4. Romans 1:16; 15:27.
5. See Romans 1:2; 3:1-2; also 15:4.
6. See Romans 3:29-30; 8:21; 11:32.

"gospel of God" and (2) the continuing need to be faithful to its Jewish character and roots.

Far better than most of his contemporaries, Paul knew the Eastern half of the Roman empire. He lived and worked in a number of its cities. He could not have communicated with its inhabitants as effectively as he did had he not known their language, customs, hopes, and fears. Nor can we proceed far in the study of his letters without needing to take into account the occurrence of terms, techniques, and notions drawn from his familiarity with the Greco-Roman world. Still, the exploration of such details lies beyond our purpose here. The underlying framework remains, for Paul, Jewish in its origins. It includes his convictions about the goodness of God the Creator and the consequent derived goodness of the created order; an understanding of creation's present disorder, not in tragic terms, as the surfacing of flaws or tensions inherent in the nature of the cosmos, but in moral and religious terms, as the consequence of culpable creaturely unfaithfulness toward God; the implacable hostility of God toward the evil that mars the goodness of what he has made; the ultimate triumph of the Good assured by the conjunction of God's own irrepressible goodness and his irresistible right arm. Paul's Christian understanding of divine "redemption" fits perfectly within these horizons, though it certainly required modifications of other Jewish beliefs. Our task in the pages that follow will be to recover the main lines of Paul's distinctive statement of this "Jewish-Christian" worldview.[7]

---

7. The "Jewish-Christian" worldview referred to here and in the pages that follow is that defined, as in the paragraph above, by the following convictions: God is good, and so is his creation; evil represents an inappropriate and disruptive response on the part of moral beings to what is good; the triumph of the Good is ultimately assured by the character of God. That Judaism and Christianity have developed in quite different ways, with different emphases, may well be obscured by unqualified references to a "Judaeo-Christian" tradition or heritage. The Jewish origin of the central Christian (and Pauline) convictions listed above is the sole point of my own references to the "Jewish-Christian" worldview. (The quotation marks are intended to limit the term to the technical sense here defined.)

Chapter 2

Intuitions of Goodness —
and Divine *Tzedakah*

ROMANS 1:16-17

THAT LIFE — all life — is meaningful and good, and that evil distorts and disrupts the good and cries out to be set right: these convictions are fundamental to the "Jewish-Christian" worldview[1] of which Paul is a notable exponent. They are not self-evident today. In this chapter a general discussion of the differences in horizons will be followed by a look at the theme of underlying goodness in the biblical book of Psalms. We will then see, in conclusion, how that vision provides the framework for the Pauline manifesto in Romans 1:16-17.

Love — and the Nature of Things

We may begin with a parable.

Barb and Bob knew each other for years before they "discovered" one another. The details of the "discovery" need not concern us here. Barb and Bob themselves feel that what has happened to them is utterly unique in the annals of human history, and in a sense, of course, they are right: Barb is unique, so is Bob, and so perforce must be their relationship. But though we grant the point with goodwill — we were,

1. On the phrase, see Chapter One, n. 7.

after all, once young ourselves — we do them no injustice when we insist that, broadly speaking, what has happened to them *has* happened to others before; that, for all its novelty in detail, there is a certain predictability about many aspects of the relationship; that the whole experience is sufficiently common in sufficiently significant ways to warrant the dusting off of a well-worn tag: Barb and Bob have "fallen in love," and even those who know neither Barb nor Bob, when they hear the news, have a fair idea of what has taken place.

Indeed, whether or not Barb and Bob care to acknowledge it, their mutual "discovery" bears an unmistakable resemblance to that of a male and female albatross whom we will call Jack and Jill. Jill, on returning to the land of her birth, is beset by many males, all craving her attention; but she finds herself attracted to Jack. A certain formality of gesture and speech, both awkward and tense with excitement, characterizes their initial introductions: their attachment will be lifelong, its beginnings must not be rushed. Introductions are followed by gentle caressing, then a dance: formal, predictable, yet reaching a feverish ecstasy before subsiding into the contentment of the mutual knowledge that they are a pair. Still, Jack and Jill will separate for a season without mating. Their reunion is marked again by both excitement and formality, though now, at the end of their courtship dance, they mate, then prepare to take up the shared responsibilities of parenting.

We leave them to their duties and return to Barb and Bob. Their new relationship has transformed their lives. Their pursuit of work and education is now purposeful, focused on making possible their life together. The most trite of occasions has taken on meaning — provided they can share it with each other. Even separation from one another has a different character than times they used to spend on their own: "absence" is not the same as "aloneness." Nor would we be mistaken in thinking Barb and Bob more beautiful human beings than they were before: more happy, certainly, but also more generous, more patient, more considerate. That love is blind, attributing spectacular virtues to spectacularly ordinary people, is not, after all, the whole truth. Virtue may also be summoned into being by love.

So much for the parable. In view of the pluralism — the multiculturalism — of our society, you would not, of course, permit that the story be given but a single interpretation. Will . . . *two* do?

On one view,[2] Barb and Bob are in the process of inventing the terms of their own relationship. Others have had similar experiences; human physiology has seen to that. Still, in a mechanical universe whose only meaning or value is human in origin, nothing in the accidents of human physiology or in the experience of other human beings can dictate to our pair what *their* attitudes or behavior ought to be. Admittedly, some things that they might choose to do will be followed by predictable consequences, and we would not think them wise to overlook such factors when they make their choices. Some of their potential activities impinge upon society as a whole; in such matters they will need to take into account the law of the land (they must, for example, assume responsibility for their off-spring). Still, if humans are autonomous — if they are "on their own," so to speak, in the universe — pursuing their own ends in a value-neutral world, then Barb and Bob are largely free to make (and break) their own rules, to create a relationship that suits only them, and to enjoy it as long as they mutually choose to do so.

But for many people of other lands and ages (and for many people still today), the suggestion that Barb and Bob are inventing something new in an unstructured, value-free universe would be counterintuitive and nonsensical. The intuitions of such people are guided in part by widespread familiarity with what Barb and Bob have experienced (indeed, the pattern, as we have noted, extends beyond humans to include Jack and Jill Albatross as well). People of the modern West may be inclined to dismiss the significance of the pattern, attributing it to the accidents of animal physiology and insisting that, at any rate, Barb and Bob must be left free to create the terms of their own relationship, to determine what is best for themselves. Historically, however, many people, observing animal and human physiology and its transparent fittedness for the perpetuation of species, have seen evidence of a design in nature — and of the wisdom of a designer. They have sensed, further, that a design that underlies and defines the nature of our being must place limits on what behavior is fitting, or most fulfilling, for humans. To this latter point we will return in due course.

---

2. The point of view here summarized is chosen because (1) it is common enough in our day, and (2) it offers a sharp and illuminating contrast to the thinking of Paul. That there are other and intermediary positions is not denied; but it lies outside our purpose to develop them.

For our immediate purposes, however, an even more crucial in-
tuition than that of design has been that of nature's inherent goodness.
Barb and Bob's love is not only nature's convenient way of assuring the
propagation of the species. It is itself a Good Thing, a cause for celebration in its own right. Nor has its goodness been thought of as con-
fined to that of sensual pleasure (though sensual pleasure belongs to its
more obvious enticements and rewards). Indeed, the goodness of love
is commonly considered to be more purely expressed, and more last-
ingly felt, in the mutual support of lovers through the monotonies of
quotidian tasks and the pains and struggles of hard times. Furthermore,
if the awakening of a human being to the reality and goodness of
another's existence and the subordinating of individual goals and interests to the higher values of mutuality are Good Things, the same must
presumably be said of Jack and Jill's adoption of a life with a similar
pattern. Humans may bring to their experience a degree of conscious-
ness and a capacity for articulation that *this* Jack and Jill will never
possess; but the latter, too, know, delight in, and sacrifice for the goodness of a shared existence. In short, humans (and other species of
animals) appear to many to have been designed in such a way as to
entice them to the Goodness of mutuality: "It is not good that the man
should be alone."[3] We can, on this interpretation, only rejoice that Barb
and Bob have come to discover and experience something fundamental
to the nature of their humanity. But (still on this interpretation) we can
only shake our heads at their hubris should they imagine that they are
themselves the creators of purpose and goodness in a structureless,
value-free universe.

According to the first view, we live in a world thrown together by
the chance assembly of particles of matter. The suitedness to survival
that we discern in its life-forms must represent, not the work of some
supernatural designer, but merely those random combinations of
globules that proved capable of perpetuating themselves. To speak of
the "beauty" or "goodness" of "all that is" or of any of its parts is merely
a poetic (or naïve) way of saying that *we* find particular conglomerations
of globules pleasing or useful to us. Whatever patterns that nature has
thrown together can be reshaped into something better corresponding
to human preference or convenience. After all, a nature with no purpose

3. Genesis 2:18.

of its own provides only raw material for purpose-driven human beings. Nor can there be any inherent "rightness" or "wrongness" in the nature of "things," haphazard and unstructured as "things" are.

In principle, then, humans are free to choose what they think best or most desirable for themselves. Since their choices will be diverse, the greatest premium will be placed on the virtue of tolerance (that is, on the ability to live with people who choose differently than we), whereas a great vice will be seen in any attempt to impose one's own choices on others. Any constraint placed upon us not of our choosing (apart from those required for mutual coexistence) can only be an arbitrary, unjustifiable expression of a "will to power," a desire to dominate, on the part of the constrainer. (Those whose thinking is governed by such a worldview can only view would-be "apostles" with grave suspicion!)

On the second worldview sketched above, however, trouble springs precisely from the human presumption that we are free to remake the world to our own specifications, that nature itself has no order or goodness that we need to respect. Words like "beauty" and "goodness," while reflecting human perceptions, put us on the right track: they express an awareness of a presence and purpose in nature not our own to which we appropriately respond with wonder and appreciation. Nor, on this view, can the language of "right" and "wrong," at its root, be the arbitrary invention of human beings desirous of imposing their will upon others. However subject to abuse and distortion such language may be, it is nonetheless grounded in a proper sense that there are adequate and inadequate, appropriate and disastrously inappropriate, ways of responding to the reality of life in our world. Obviously, human choice is pivotal to this worldview, as it is to the first. The distinctiveness of human beings, however, lies here not in any supposed power to shape an unstructured world to their liking, but in their capacity to fathom, affirm, and celebrate the goodness of the created order. They are thus called upon to add a human dimension to the goodness and glory of the whole — though, alas, the capacity for affirming and celebrating the Good inevitably opens to humans the contrary possibility as well: they *can* refuse to acknowledge or respect any good in the cosmos but that of personal ambition and pleasure. The self-absorption of the latter choice breeds rivalry, distrust, conflict, and destruction.

The worldviews here sketched are in fundamental tension with each other. Contemporary confidence that the "scientific method" can resolve the dispute is misplaced. Science may observe nature's conduciveness to various kinds of life; it has no instrument for determining whether life is good. Science may note the patterns or the chaos apparent in the fraction of reality open to its observation; but its grasp of "all that is" can never be sufficient to justify claims about the structure, or lack of structure, of the whole; nor, if there is structure, can the observations of science distinguish between a mechanically functioning order and an intelligently formed design. Science can tell us how to exploit nature; it is silent to what extent we should. To evaluate the fundamental human issues raised by a comparison of worldviews, we will need to summon human resources both deeper and older than the "scientific method."

The Goodness That Underlies All — in the Psalms

In the book of Psalms, we repeatedly encounter the insistence that "the Lord is good"; we are even offered the exquisite invitation to "taste and see" how good he is.[4] One might have thought that God was simply good by definition: Is it not, after all, a prerogative of the Creator to decide what is good, and what bad, in the first place? Still, the psalmists believed that they were making a significant statement. Frequently they have in mind the *kindness* shown by the Lord to those in need. Psalm 107 summons all humanity to praise the Lord for his goodness, and develops the point by declaring that he comes to the aid of the lost, the imprisoned, the sick and hungry, the storm-tossed. In short, those in need who cry out to the Lord are believed to experience firsthand his "goodness."[5]

God's goodness is also, and more fundamentally, thought to be reflected in creation itself, in the goodness of life in a world perceived as splendidly and benevolently ordered.[6] The chaotic seas have been put in their place, thank God![7] So have the mountains, and they are not

---

4. Psalm 34:8. Note that biblical references use the numbering of chapters and verses found in the standard English versions.

5. See also Psalm 31:19; 86:5.

6. See Psalm 65:9-13; 104:27-28; 145:9-10.

7. See Psalm 33:7; 65:7; 89:9.

about to move anywhere, praise the Lord![8] The springs and the valleys, the grass and the trees have their place.[9] So do animals, storm winds, rain, snow and hail, the sun, the moon, and all the stars; indeed, God has given to each of the stars not only a place but also a name.[10] All is perfectly ordered and providentially sustained. The world, we are told, is "full of the dependable love of the Lord."[11]

We may well find curious the way the psalmists can abstract, out of all the ambiguities of lived experience, this *un*ambiguous portrayal of the glories of the created order. The psalmists knew famine, disease, violence, and death. And yet, in some of the psalms at least, no trace of evil of any kind is a part of the picture. The focus, the single-mindedness, the purity of their vision is impressive. On a similar note, the psalmists boldly summon humanity of all shapes and sizes and ages and nations to respond with appropriate praise to the Lord. Yet in their day, the "Lord" was acknowledged and worshiped only by the people of a petty kingdom of the Levant, themselves not exclusive in their devotion. Nothing of this clouds the psalmists' horizons.

> Kings of the earth, and all people;
>   princes, and all judges of the earth:
> Both young men, and maidens;
>   old men, and children:
> Let them praise the name of the Lord:
>   for his name alone is excellent.[12]

To dismiss such texts as naïve would only show our own naïveté. Rather, they are an affirmation that ultimately, fundamentally, creation is good, and the Creator deserving of universal praise; that the reality of evil is *not* ultimate, but secondary and parasitic, a disorder brought about by inappropriate responses to the goodness of the fundamental order. Consequently, the psalmists were determined that, for the moment at least, they were not going to allow secondary distractions,

evil

---

8. See Psalm 65:6; 104:5-9.
9. Psalm 104:10-17.
10. Psalm 147:4; 148:3-10.
11. Psalm 33:5.
12. Psalm 148:11-13, King James Version.

however distressing, or the blindness of others, however widespread or obtuse, to interfere with their celebration of the essential goodness of life in God's creation.

Still more fundamentally, the psalmists found good, and profoundly satisfying, not simply the manifest works of the Lord, but also, and at a deeper level, a sense of his very presence. To worship in the courtyard of the Lord's temple was for them to experience his goodness in an exhilarating, almost palpable way, so that a single day there was treasured more than a thousand anywhere else.[13] There one "beheld" his "beauty" and "sang for joy" to the "living God."[14] To "dwell in the house of the Lord forever" was to know "goodness and mercy" all one's days.[15] Separation from God's house left one faint, longing as a hart for flowing streams, parched as in a "dry and weary land" without water.[16] It provoked the cry:

> O send out your light and your truth;
>   let them lead me;
> let them bring me to your holy hill
>   and to your dwelling.
> Then will I go to the altar of God,
>   to God my exceeding joy;
> and I will praise you with the harp,
>   O God, my God.[17]

The writer of the incomparable Psalm 139 goes further: the divine presence encompasses him wherever he may go.

> If I take the wings of the morning,
>   and dwell in the uttermost parts of the sea;
> Even there shall thy hand lead me,
>   and thy right hand shall hold me . . .
>   when I awake, I am still with thee.[18]

13. Psalm 84:10; also 65:4.
14. Psalm 27:4; 84:2.
15. So ends the familiar Psalm 23.
16. Psalm 42:1; 63:1.
17. Psalm 43:3-4, New Revised Standard Version.
18. Psalm 139:9-10, 18, King James Version.

Again, the psalmists who found such satisfaction in God's "face" were fully aware of the darker aspects of life: is there anywhere a literature that more profoundly probes the lot of the despised, the slandered, the despondent, those ravaged by disease or war? God's ways are often disturbingly mysterious even for the psalmists. They feel that at times he has "hidden" his "face," and they cannot understand why.[19] Nonetheless, what prevails in the end is the unshakable faith in their bones, whatever the fate of their flesh, that underlying all is goodness, beyond human comprehension but still worthy of human trust: a goodness not only worth clinging to when all else fails, but more precious by far than anything else one might desire.

> Whom have I in heaven but you?
>> And there is nothing on earth
>>> that I desire other than you.
> My flesh and my heart may fail,
>> but God is the strength of my heart
>>> and my portion forever.[20]

Divine goodness cannot, however, fail in the end, nor remain ambiguous forever: divine *tzedakah* will see to that. This Hebrew word is commonly rendered "righteousness," a term that captures part of what the psalmists mean to convey: that God keeps his word and lives up to his obligations, and that his obligations include that of enforcing the moral order, of seeing to it that both righteous and wicked receive their due recompense. But the term "righteousness" has fallen into disuse and does not in any case sufficiently suggest the element of *goodness* so obviously present in psalmic texts summoning the universe to celebrate God's *tzedakah*. In such verses the term refers to the faithfulness of God toward his creation or his people, a faithfulness that moves him to intervene, to set things wonderfully right, when they have gone disastrously awry. It is the reassertion of God's goodness seen in the restoration of order to a disturbed creation, of peace and prosperity to a distressed people. *Tzedakah* in this sense is close in meaning to "salvation." What *tzedakah* adds to the "reassertion of goodness" and even

---

19. Psalm 13:1; 89:46.
20. Psalm 73:25-26, New Revised Standard Version.

"salvation" is the implication that God, in the process, is living up to his responsibility and role as God, that he is proving himself loyal to the commitments he undertook when he first made the world good, or adopted Israel as his people.

> O sing unto the Lord a new song;
> for he hath done marvellous things:
> his right hand, and his holy arm,
> hath gotten him the victory.
> The Lord hath made known his salvation:
> his righteousness *[tzedakah]* hath he openly showed
> in the sight of the heathen.
> He hath remembered his mercy and his truth
> toward the house of Israel:
> all the ends of the earth have seen
> the salvation of our God. . . .
> Let the sea roar, and the fulness thereof;
> the world, and they that dwell therein.
> Let the floods clap their hands:
> let the hills be joyful together
> Before the Lord; for he cometh
> to judge the earth:
> with righteousness *[tzedek]* shall he judge the world,
> and the people with equity.[21]

Similar uses of the term *tzedakah* (also in close parallel with "salvation") occur in the later chapters of Isaiah, as the prophet proclaims how a despondent people in exile are about to experience afresh the divine goodness.[22] Significantly for our purposes, in speaking of the proclamation of such good news, the prophet uses a verb that is rendered in Greek *euangelizesthai,*[23] related to the Greek noun *euangelion* (whence the English "evangelist"), which, in turn, in the English New Testament is translated "gospel."

---

21. Psalm 98:1-3, 7-9, King James Version.
22. Isaiah 45:8; 46:12-13; 51:6.
23. Isaiah 40:9; 52:7; 61:1.

... and in Paul

When Paul, in turning from his commission to "proclaim good news" *(euangelizesthai)*[24] to a summary manifesto of what it is he proclaims, declares that the "gospel" *(euangelion)* brings God's "salvation" and demonstrates divine "righteousness,"[25] he is interpreting the significance of Jesus within the framework provided by the Jewish vision of divine goodness that we have sketched in this chapter. God is good, and so, necessarily, is his creation. His *tzedakah*[26] demands that, in a world gone awry, God will restore, in some manifestly divine fashion, the goodness of what he has made.

24. Romans 1:15.
25. Romans 1:16-17.
26. The term in Hebrew has taken on a more limited sense: human liberality, almsgiving, charity. I use the term in the sense given it in the passages from the Psalms and Isaiah cited above.

Chapter 3

War against Goodness

ROMANS 1:18-32

NO DOUBT all of us have a partiality for one or more of the "Seven Deadly Sins"; still, people of the modern West seldom speak of "sin." Paul did not share our hesitation. Our first task in this chapter will be to explore and account for the difference in sensibilities.

We may begin with reflections about the roots of the modern discomfort with, and a possible modern approach to, "Jewish-Christian"[1] notions of wrongdoing. We will then look briefly at the morality of the biblical book of Proverbs before focusing on significant features of Paul's own depiction of human sin in Romans 1:18-32.

The Modern West and "Sin"

The very notion of wrongdoing is approached by many moderns with misgivings. Several contributing factors are worth noting.

1. We in the modern West insist on the freedom of individuals to choose for themselves, to pursue their own goals and values. Complete freedom of choice we know to be impracticable in a world whose air we must share with others (that is, in the world as we know it, we need to take some account of others' needs and desires at the same time as we pursue

1. On the term, see Chapter One, n. 7.

the satisfaction of our own) and whose surface, should we test it by a leap from any great height, provides little cushion (that is, in the world as we know it, a consideration of predictable consequences will, for most of us, quickly exclude a fair number of potential choices). Nonetheless, we remain suspicious of attempts to restrict our options. Many moderns resist the assertion of traditional morality that certain ways in which they might choose to express themselves are inherently "wrong."

2. Closely related is the contemporary insistence that people must not impose their moral standards or values on others, or be "judgmen-tal." Again, the implication seems to be that it is not for any of us to say that what other people choose to do is either "right" or "wrong."

3. Historically, religious conviction was one of the roots of the modern West's insistence upon individual freedom. A central element, for example, in the beginnings of the "American experiment" was the demand of different groups to be allowed to worship as they deemed right. At issue for them was not whether or not there was a right way to worship (the answer to this question tended to be Yes), but whether the powers-that-be in the land-that-was had rightly divined it (the answer to this question tended to be No). "Right" and "wrong" there were, but where citizens believed themselves to be in the right and their rulers to be in the wrong, constraints imposed by the latter upon the former were liable to be seen as violating their conscience; hence the religious fervor with which freedom of worship (for example) was demanded. Many people, moreover, are convinced that religious beliefs and moral conduct, if they are to represent truly religious or moral acts, *must* be freely chosen by the individual, not the result of mere compli-ance with the state's demands. There is thus, in the demand for freedom in matters of faith and morals, nothing either in principle or in its history inconsistent with very firm beliefs that there are "rights" to be chosen, and "wrongs" to be avoided, in both of these spheres.

Nonetheless, in societies where a diversity of conviction is per-mitted and no particular perspective on matters of religion or morals is allowed a platform in the schools and other public institutions, the language of "right" and "wrong" that characterizes strongly held con-victions easily comes to appear ill-suited to public discourse — and suspect in people's minds. Children taught in religious homes of the fundamental importance of religious beliefs and practices, or of reli-giously grounded moral standards, can hardly avoid wondering how "fundamental" such matters can be when they are either studiously avoided in the classroom or brought up only to make the point that "opinions differ" and "different views must be respected." When demands for freedom and for tolerance of diversity dominate public discussion, the perception is readily fostered that "one way of looking at things is as good as another"; that the adoption of a particular perspective can hardly be a matter of urgency; and that insistence upon language of "right" and "wrong" is the hallmark of the narrow-minded.

4. The misgivings about the language of "right" and "wrong" noted in the preceding paragraph are the (perhaps unintended) product of the relegation of religion and moral conviction, by both law and etiquette, to private spheres. Yet the worldview of many moderns itself leaves little place for such language, at least in its traditional usage. Where nature is thought to show only mechanical order, morality may be dismissed as arbitrary convention or suspected as the invention of one class of people to promote its own interests by controlling the conduct of others. Viewed more positively, the moral sense of humans may be thought of as an asset acquired in the process of human evolution, serving to promote human survival and well-being. Alternatively, conventions of morality may be regarded as a product of human culture honed over millennia into a fairly dependable guide to the welfare of the individual within society. Still, even these more favorable understandings of morality convey, at best, a reason for thinking it prudent or beneficial (in some sense) to conform with morality's dictates. It is not clear why one is "right" to conform either to a useful convention or to an evolutionary development suited to the survival of the species; and in what sense would one be "wrong" if one refused to do so? The terms have lost (on any of these current views) much of their traditional force.

5. Finally, moderns know that heredity and environment greatly affect human attitudes and actions. Even where we cannot but look upon certain kinds of conduct with disapproval, we readily accede to the reminder that a number of factors for which the culprits in question bear no responsibility have contributed to (if not determined) their behavior. Is it appropriate, then, to use the language of "right" and "wrong," with its connotations of "praiseworthy" and "blameworthy"?

And yet, for all of our misgivings, we have not dispensed with the language of "right" and "wrong" — and, in the end, we would not want to do so. Most of us, if pressed, would insist that Hitler, or Stalin, or the classroom bully of our primary school days made a fair number of choices that were not merely imprudent, unwise, or nonbeneficial, but — in some fundamental, not merely conventional sense — *wrong*. Teachers today are wont to insist that they are not imposing *their* moral standards on students; but if Johnny persists in seeing nothing amiss in cheating, or in shutting up cats inside automatic driers and turning on the machines, many of us would hope that his teacher will succeed in introducing Johnny to some (rather traditional) notions of moral behavior. For all our awareness of the impact of heredity and environment (our legal systems continue to assume that most people should be held responsible for most of what they do;) so, too, does our everyday conversation. And for all our assurance that we can account for human moral sentiments by means of some such explanation as those given above, we find that the explanations fail to yield satisfactory answers to moral dilemmas that persist in arising. "How much attention *ought* I to give a senile parent, or a handicapped child?" The question may not occur to people naturally kind or to those notoriously self-absorbed. But it occurs to others and is likely to remain an issue, urgent and unresolved, even if we convince ourselves that the sentiments urging us to act are the product of a quirk of evolution or of arbitrary human convention.

Enough has been said of the modern ambivalence toward language of "right" and "wrong" to provide a background against which we may explore the very different thinking of the apostle Paul. The task of seeing "sin" through his eyes must surely rank among our most formidable undertakings. Nor will definitions, however precise, even begin to evoke for modern readers Paul's sense of sin. Narrative (in this case, a series of short narratives) provides (again) our best starting-point.

A Modern Approximation of "Sin"

First, then, a series of related parables.[2]

1. Ashley and Chrystal, exchange students in Paris, spend thirty-

---

2. Verisimilitude, it should be remembered, is not essential to the genre. Caricature — introduced to make a point — is quite in order. Resemblances between the figures of my parables and real live people of my own or the reader's acquaintance are strictly coincidental.

two and a half minutes in the halls of the Louvre, chatting and giggling all the while about the boys they left behind them. They later report that the museum had a lot of paintings.

2. Brandon enters his brother Jason's room, sees it transformed into a boyish fort, stifles the thought that his own room is not nearly as neat, and trashes in seconds what his brother had spent hours in constructing. Called to account for his action, Brandon demands how he was supposed to know that the stupid mop was supposed to be a stupid flag, that the stupid pile of books was supposed to be a stupid tower, that the stupid sticks were supposed to be stupid soldiers. No one had told *him*. He was, most unfairly (he felt), sent to his room.

3. Ashley and Chrystal, upon entering a cathedral of staggering beauty, spend six and three-quarter minutes telling jokes as they aimlessly wander the aisles. Outside one of its chapels, they are requested either to be a little quieter or to talk outside, since a funeral is in progress. They leave in a bit of a huff. Asked later what they had seen that day, they forget to mention Notre Dame.

4. Like many boys, Brandon likes catching butterflies, frogs, and snakes. Like some boys, Brandon likes cutting them up with his knife.

5. Ashley and Chrystal are taken by their hosts to the Swiss Alps. At the Matterhorn, at Lake Geneva, at countless other sites of breathtaking beauty, the breath of Ashley and Chrystal is devoted to nonstop trivial conversation. To their credit, they do remember later that there are a "whole lot of mountains" in Switzerland, though they are decidedly of the opinion that, if you have seen one mountain, you have seen them all.

6. Brandon, now in his mid-teens and brandishing a bottle, saunters across a Little League baseball diamond, pretending not to notice that a game is in progress. He kicks second base into right field, makes fun of the "squirt" who retrieves it, showers the leftfielder with the remains of his bottle. Challenged to move on, Brandon snorts that *he* always thought it was a free country, that he will leave when he feels like it. The feeling apparently comes over him at the very moment when a police cruiser is seen to pass slowly by the field.

7. Ashley and Chrystal return home to New Jersey. At the airport, waiting to see them, are their parents, who had worked long and hard, but proudly, to send their daughters to France. Ashley and Chrystal, engrossed in trivial conversation, initially walk past their parents in the

lounge. Hearing their names, they half-turn their heads to inquire, "Where's the car?"

8. At dusk, several hours after the game, Brandon returns to a now-abandoned field and discovers a catcher's mitt that was left behind. It never occurs to Brandon to take the glove; what would *he* do with a catcher's mitt? Instead, he brandishes his penknife and cuts the glove to shreds. He is about to leave the field when he bumps into an anxious father and son running toward the field. Sizing up the situation, Brandon anticipates their outcry with a shrug: "You leave it, you lose it."

9. High school days over, needing something to do, Ashley and Chrystal decide to become social workers. One of their first assignments takes them to assess the needs of a young widow with three small children recently thrust into Ashley and Chrystal's community from a war zone in the third world. Ashley and Chrystal spend fifty-one and a half minutes of their hour-long visit in wide-ranging chatter with each other. They later report that the refugees will probably be needing food.

10. Several years later, again at dusk, Brandon comes upon a little girl playing by herself in a park near some trees. "Shouldn't have left her alone," he mutters.

In at least the later stories, readers will agree, something is not quite (or not at all) as it should be. The *root* of our feeling is scarcely some sense that laws are being broken; apart from, presumably, the tenth episode and, possibly, the sixth, the law is not even an issue. Nor would most of us readily think of moral rules that have been infringed. We could, in some cases, come up with a rule the observance of which would have led Ashley, Brandon, or Chrystal (hereafter ABC) to behave differently. Had, for example, AC been reminded of some such principle as "Gratitude should be shown toward benefactors" (or even "Honor your father and your mother"), they might not have shown the thoughtlessness of episode seven. But for most of us, such a rule would represent a secondary attempt to articulate and to generalize a more spontaneous feeling about what is proper in a situation like that in the episode. The rule, however serviceable, is not the *source* of our moral sentiment.

On the other hand, to the extent that we are prepared to insist that our moral sentiments in these cases are warranted, we *are* saying that the scope of behavior allowed by human freedom is much wider than the range of actions that we deem appropriate. AC may be "free" to ignore their parents; but they are inconsiderate if they do so. And could they not have responded more sympathetically to the widow in episode nine? Perhaps B is "free" to cut to shreds a catcher's mitt that he finds; but he *must* have been aware that the mitt meant a lot to someone, and that his act of destruction served no purpose. And — forgetting the illegality — how *could* he treat the innocence, or the very life, of a child as having no value beyond the gratification of a moment's destructive urge?

Common to each of the episodes is the self-absorption of ABC. B's self-preoccupation is pernicious in ways that AC's is not. Still, when confronted with some reality not of their own making, they all proceed at the least to ignore it, at the worst to belittle it, trample on it, abuse it. Little League games and cathedrals, a boyish fort and the Matterhorn, butterflies, parents, a child at play and a widow: these realities external to ABC elicit from them either no response whatever (in AC's case) or (in B's) a perverse insistence on his freedom to do as he pleases. AC, we may feel, need to grow up; B, to change his ways. All three need to open their eyes to the reality of a world much bigger than themselves.

Sin in Proverbs

The book of Proverbs is replete with expressions of moral sentiment. Yet these sentiments are seldom related to any code of moral law; in that respect they are like our own. And a premise underlying the argument of the whole book is that humans have wide powers to do as they choose: in an important sense they are (as we are wont to emphasize) "free." But the argument built in Proverbs upon that premise is that some of our potential choices are appropriate, right, and wise while others are inappropriate and disastrous. We did not make the world; we are constantly confronted with realities not of our choosing or design; and how we respond to these realities betrays our character and ultimately — the world being what it is — determines our fate.

Much of the book is made up, not of direct moral counsel, but simply of observations and reminders that in the world as we know it, certain kinds of behavior entail certain predictable consequences. The point, whether implicit or explicit, is that the wise will bear this in mind, while the foolish, by definition, do not. Providing security for the loans of people you hardly know is not a wise thing to do.[3] Inactivity at seedtime and harvest invites disaster (even the ants know better!).[4] So does a refusal to listen to the advice of others.[5] So do a quick temper, a loose tongue, pride and excessive self-assurance, addiction to strong drink, and, indeed, the consumption of too much honey.[6] Of course humans are "free" in all of these matters to ignore what experience has long since discovered about the nature of reality. If they do, however, they will pay the price.

The cause-and-effect pattern in the instances given above is no doubt apparent even today. But the list in Proverbs goes on. Wrong, wicked, foolish, and baneful behavior includes slander and gossip, cheating in business, accepting bribes, charging exorbitant interest, adultery, cruelty to animals, turning a deaf ear to the cries of the needy.[7] The point, for Proverbs, is the same in these cases as in the preceding. We do not live in an unstructured, value-neutral world where we are free to decide what is best for ourselves. The world — by divine wisdom — has been given an order that is good, promoting our life and well-being. Human freedom (Proverbs itself does not use the term) amounts to the power to choose its response to the divinely imposed order. We can respect and celebrate and live in harmony with it by being honest in speech, fair and compassionate in our dealings with others, diligent in doing what needs to be done, reverent toward God: a course of life that is "righteous" and "wise" and conducive to our own good. Or we can refuse to recognize any good that we ourselves do not define and that does not have us as its focus — thus defying the order in which we cannot help but live. Proverbs' phrase for those who make such a choice is that they are "wise in their own eyes."[8] Their path, the book insists, can only end in disaster. Proverbs uses all of the resources at its disposal to encourage the choosing of the good.

Three further features of the argument of Proverbs merit brief mention here.

1. Proverbs frequently speaks as though the moral order itself recoils and brings disaster upon those who flout and abuse it. Such

---

3. Proverbs 11:15.
4. Proverbs 6:6-11; 20:4.
5. Proverbs 12:1; 15:32.
6. Proverbs 14:17; 13:3; 11:2; 28:26; 20:1; 25:16.
7. Proverbs 10:18; 11:13; 11:1; 17:23; 28:8; 6:24-35; 12:10; 21:13.
8. Proverbs 3:7.

people will eat the fruit of their own way; their perversity will be their own death.[9] Other texts, however, speak of God as overseeing and enforcing the moral order. The good obtain favor from him, whereas he condemns those who concoct evil.[10] The two perspectives are quite compatible: the moral order, put in place and supervised by a righteous God, perfectly expresses his love of righteousness and hatred of wickedness by promoting the well-being of the righteous and assuring the calamitous end of the wicked.

2. In such a world, taking God into account (literally, "fearing" him) is the first and most essential step in coming to terms with reality.[11] If God is the Maker of all and human destiny is in his hands, then it does indeed follow that our most appropriate and urgent response to the reality that confronts us is to give God his due.

3. From the perspective of other biblical traditions and later Jewish and Christian thought, the equation that we find in Proverbs of material prosperity with wise and righteous living, and of earthly calamity with the path of wickedness, is too simplistic. The point of Proverbs — that we find · ourselves confronted with a reality and an order not of our making, and that we may respond in appropriate or inappropriate ways — is central to Jewish and Christian visions of reality. That our choices, frequently enough, bear fit and immediate consequences is also a common insistence. But we need only cite the book of Job in the Hebrew Scriptures and the Beatitudes in the Christian[12] to remind ourselves that Jews and Christians alike would concede that divine enforcement of the moral order has a rationale and a timetable not transparent to human view. Nor is Proverbs itself insensitive to the point. Together with texts that relate fearing the Lord to fullness of barns[13] are others that claim that it is "better" to be poor than dishonest, "better" to be upright and poor than crooked and rich.[14] In what sense *better*? Proverbs has no vocabulary to develop the point. There is a "rightness" in God's world. In the end, it is somehow "better" to live in harmony with that rightness under any conditions than to defy it, for whatever apparent gain.

9. See, e.g., Proverbs 1:31-32.
10. See Proverbs 12:2.
11. More literally, it is "the beginning of knowledge" (Proverbs 1:7).
12. See Matthew 5:3-12.
13. Proverbs 3:7-10.
14. Proverbs 19:22; 28:6.

. . . and in Paul

Paul's depiction of human sinfulness in Romans 1:18-32 is essentially a restatement of perspectives apparent already in Proverbs. Here we will largely be content to note the parallels.

1. Paul does not refer in this passage to divine law. Human "sinfulness" here is a matter of willfully inappropriate responses to reality, not the transgression of a specified moral code.

2. If sin is inappropriate response to reality, the fundamental human sin (for Paul as for Proverbs) is the failure to respond appropriately to the Creator of all that is. Those who are in the presence of awesome natural or artistic beauty and yet fail to respond with wonder betray their own self-absorption and insensitivity; similarly, for Paul, to enjoy life in a world created and ordered by divine goodness without responding with thanks to God is unnatural, perverse, sinful — and the root of all other sins.[15] The latter represent a refusal to live in harmony with some aspect of the divine order of creation. They follow inevitably from a refusal to give recognition to the Creator himself. For Paul, sin, at its root, is something far more egregious than the violation of various norms; it represents the rejection and insulting of a Person — indeed, of the One to whom humans owe everything they are and have and who himself wills their own well-being.

3. To be properly "sinful," human "sinfulness" must be inexcusable. Paul stresses that humans refuse to acknowledge God despite having the evidence for his power and deity before their eyes, and that people sin in sundry ways in spite of an awareness that envy, murder, strife, deceit, and the like are wrong.[16] Human sin thus goes beyond the wrongfulness of individual acts to include in each case a "suppression" of, a willful blindness toward, the truth of human dependence upon God.[17] We did not make our world. But when we defy its order and goodness with our greed, malice, slander, and faithlessness, we assume the right of creators to define the terms of their own existence. Such is the lie — the "disobeying of the truth"[18] — implicit in every sin. Paul also claims, however, that such sin affects human minds. To sin against the light one has can only lead to the

---

15. Romans 1:19-23, 28.
16. Romans 1:18-21, 29-32.
17. Romans 1:18, 28.
18. Romans 2:8.

darkening of one's powers of perception (no doubt because, in the inevitable process of justifying their conduct to themselves and others, sinners skew their own moral and religious sensibilities).[19] This point will become important in the next chapter.

4. Illustrative of the human refusal to acknowledge the created order are, for Paul, the homosexual activities of both women and men.[20] Paul knew nothing of modern constructions of such activities as expressing a genetically determined sexual "orientation" or even a psychological disorder brought on by a dysfunctional childhood. Others today would stress the personal choice involved in such activity — and in this respect they are closer to Paul. In Paul's perception and experience, homosexual activity represented an outlet for sexual energies chosen by people who paid no heed to the appropriate place of sexuality in the created order. For Paul, sexual activity was fitting within marriage;[21] indeed, he saw the natural desire of one sex for union with the other as properly attracting them to marry.[22] On this score he was merely articulating in his day the divine sanction given to marriage in the Hebrew Scriptures: God created humanity as "male and female," intending — for their own well-being — that a man and a woman should become "one flesh," thus providing companionship for each other and offspring to "fill the earth."[23] Hence, for Paul, to indulge sexual passion outside of marriage, or with another's spouse, is to sin:[24] one is, in effect, seizing the goods of the created order on one's own terms (that is, without the attendant commitment and responsibilities). The distortion is particularly self-evident when sexual gratification is sought with members of one's own sex.[25]

19. See Romans 1:21-22.

20. Romans 1:26-27.

21. Note the contrast in 1 Thessalonians 4:3-4 between fornication and the "holiness" and "honor" of sexual intercourse within marriage. See also 1 Corinthians 7:3-4.

22. 1 Corinthians 7:2, 9, 36. The whole passage asserts, however, Paul's conviction that exceptional circumstances should lead some people at least to adopt other priorities.

23. Genesis 1:27-28; 2:18, 24.

24. See 1 Corinthians 6:9-10, 18.

25. Note Paul's emphasis on the un*natural*ness (i.e., the opposition to the designs of nature) involved when men abandon intercourse "with women" for relations of "men with men" (Romans 1:27). The terminology rules out the suggestion that Paul faults only exploitative relationships involving males of different social status. Seeking sexual gratification with members of one's own sex is itself regarded as a sin against nature's order and design. Cf. Leviticus 18:22.

5. The very being of God responds with abhorrence to the defiance and defilement of creation's goodness: on this point the Hebrew Scriptures are united. Paul reasserts the claim with his reference to divine "wrath" against all human "ungodliness" and "wickedness" in Romans 1:18. The divine way of dealing with human "sin," as Paul describes it in Romans 1:24-31, appears to be a variant of the traditional view (amply attested in Proverbs) that the created order recoils and wreaks havoc upon those who defy it. God, Paul states, has "given up" or "abandoned" sinners to the degradation of their own sins. Those who refuse to respect and comply with the goodness of creation must live in a world marred by their own envy, murder, strife, faithlessness, heartlessness, ruthlessness. Present conditions, in Paul's eyes, are thus themselves in some measure a revelation of God's wrath — though Paul will also insist on a coming, decisive judgment.[26]

Paul does not discuss "natural" evil (disease, destructive storms, earthquakes, and the like) in this passage.[27] Nor, indeed, does it frequently appear as a problem in the corpus of the Hebrew Scriptures. His attention is focused rather on the moral evil of human beings. In claiming that such evil represents a perverse and inexcusable response to the goodness of God and of the created order, Paul implies and reasserts fundamental tenets of the "Jewish-Christian" worldview: among the creatures on God's earth, humans are distinct in their capacity for making moral choices; yet we have all done things that, we know very well, we ought not to have done. In the process we have sullied the innocence both of ourselves and of our world. To be sure, we choose our own actions. But we do so in a world in which there are appropriate responses to the reality that confronts us and others that are inappropriate. There is right and there is wrong, there is good and there is evil. And which we do makes a profound difference.

---

26. Romans 2:5-11, 16.
27. He does, however, reflect on such evil in Romans 8:19-23.

Chapter 4

Israel Joins the Fray

ROMANS 2:1–3:20

IN THE MODERN West, sentences beginning "Thou shalt not" are liable to lose their audience before they reach their end. Those who insist on freedom to define what is good for themselves are wont to regard prohibitions like those of the Ten Commandments[1] as arbitrary attempts to curtail their freedom. Clearly we need to broaden our horizons if we are to see the "law of Moses" through the eyes of a Paul. In this chapter we will consider a few general aspects relating to the propriety of law in the "Jewish-Christian" worldview,[2] proceed by noting something of the centrality of "Torah" in the book of Deuteronomy, then conclude with a summary comparison of Deuteronomy's perspective with Paul's discussion of Jews and their law in Romans 2:1–3:20.

The Place of Moral Law

Inherent in (what I have labeled) the "Jewish-Christian" view, as we have seen, is the conviction that the goodness of God elicits both appropriate and inappropriate (or sinful) responses from his creatures. In principle there can be nothing problematic in spelling out and illustrating behavior

---

1. Exodus 20:1-17; Deuteronomy 5:6-21.
2. For the sense in which I use the phrase, see Chapter One, n. 7.

that becomes, and behavior that does not become, the place of humans in God's world. If life and love, health and sustenance are all gifts from the hands of God, then wholehearted devotion to him is only fitting;[3] conversely, to withhold one's worship, or to give to any other the reverence, love, and trust that are rightly the Lord's, would be perverse.[4] An appropriate response to reality can hardly take the form of misrepresenting the actions of others[5] or of taking — or even desiring — for oneself what others' work has made their own.[6] Respect for life as a gift from God to others as well as to oneself will make the thought of murder abhorrent.[7]

Marriage, moreover, in the biblical tradition, is no mere agreement between two people to live together as long as they both so choose, but itself an institution of divine creation, a project greater than themselves in which a man and a woman may nonetheless be enlisted. Since it is God who made man and woman such that they are attracted to each other, God who designed that in this way they could draw strength from their mutual companionship, and God who has ordained that their relationship should provide a fit setting for the birth and care of children, marriage is to be sanctified and celebrated as a gift to human well-being from a benevolent Creator.[8] The joys of sexual intimacy — as husband and wife become "one flesh" — are among its obvious enticements and rewards.[9] From this perspective, then, those who engage in the procreative act outside of such a relationship are involved in deceit, either by pretending to express a committed love to which they have not bound themselves (perhaps even acting in defiance of a relationship to which they have bound themselves); or by simply disregarding the created order and trivializing its gift of sexuality. Hence the prohibition of "adultery."[10] Furthermore,

all laws have a logical basis

3. Deuteronomy 6:5.

4. Deuteronomy 5:7.

5. Deuteronomy 5:20. The command forbidding one to "bear false witness" against a neighbor was intended to exclude false testimony in a legal setting. Still, slander and deception of any kind were subject to censure (see, e.g., Proverbs 10:18; 12:22), and the prohibition of "false witness" was easily interpreted as forbidding all lying.

6. Deuteronomy 5:19, 21.

7. Deuteronomy 5:17. See also Genesis 9:5-6.

8. Genesis 1:27-28; 2:18-25; Proverbs 18:22; 19:14; Matthew 19:4-6.

9. Genesis 2:24; Proverbs 5:15-20.

10. Note the esteem accorded marriage, and the warning against its violation, in

that children should honor those to whom they owe birth and breeding represents both the fulfillment of a natural obligation and the cultivation of a proper reverence for the created order within which they must live.[11]

Such "laws," within the context of the "Jewish-Christian" worldview, are not arbitrarily imposed commands curtailing human freedom any more than are the physical "demands" that people eat, drink, breathe, and sleep. Just as the human body requires sustenance and repose to prosper, so the human spirit is seen as having a capacity for communion with the Eternal, for zeal for truth, and for the giving of itself in love; and humans flourish only when these aspects of their nature are given due expression. As long as our human "will" (that which chooses what we do) is united with our reason and we cherish what we see to be true and good, then we feel no constraint when we respond to these demands of reality upon us. They become a constraint only when we insist that our behavior must reflect, not our appropriate response to creation's goodness, but the assertion of our will; that is, when we assign more importance to doing what we *choose* than to doing what is appropriate and right. For such a will, bent on its own self-assertion, on declaring its independence from the created order, the demands of reality inevitably take on the character of external coercion. But the laws of creation are an unwelcome threat only to those who choose to live in defiance of reality and who are thus, necessarily, at odds with the conditions of their own well-being.

A further conviction, however, also central to the "Jewish-Christian" view, is that such an alienation has affected all of humankind. Paul's depiction of humanity's bondage to sin is more radical than a number of other perspectives, particularly within Judaism. But the hearts of men and women are everywhere seen as having an inclination toward evil from

---

Hebrews 13:4; and see 1 Thessalonians 4:3-4. The commandment forbidding "adultery" literally prohibits a man from engaging in sexual relations with another's wife (Deuteronomy 5:18). The Mosaic law judged differently the intercourse of a man (even a married man) with an unmarried (and unengaged) woman, and a number of narratives of the Hebrew Bible suggest that such acts were not subject to significant public censure. The New Testament writings are, however, uniform in their condemnation of intercourse outside of marriage, and moral thinkers came to see such a condemnation as implicit in the creation texts of Genesis.

11. Deuteronomy 5:16.

their youth;[12] and the story of Adam and Eve,[13] though subject to different interpretations, means nothing if not that humanity suffers the bane that follows from human self-assertion.

Inevitably, humans who exercise their will in opposition to their perception of what is right attempt to patch together their now-divided personality. Human reason must justify what the human will has chosen, even at the cost of falsifying reality. The "Jewish-Christian" view insists that choices between good and evil must be made. Yet it is in principle open to the notion that the moral codes actually current in human society present the boundary between evil and good in a distorted form. Not only are such codes culturally influenced;[14] they are often blind to, or even supportive of, injustice and oppression. Such limitations are only to be expected: moral codes, after all, are formulated and passed on by human beings. The terms of the codes come to reflect not only people's tugging awareness of the obligation to do the right, but also their determination to do as they choose — and their need to legitimate their choices in terms of their (now perverted) moral sensibilities.

The Place of Law in Deuteronomy

The "Jewish-Christian" vision can account for the plurality of human moral codes and for the distorted perceptions they contain. A good God, however, can hardly be content to leave human beings in doubt, however self-induced, about what is right — and life-promoting — for them to do. The central theme of the book of Deuteronomy is that God chose to spell out the path of life for a people whose attention and indebtedness he had already secured by signal acts of divine redemption. Thus to Israel, delivered from bondage in Egypt, God revealed his "Torah." A number of its demands merely state what must be the appropriate responses that humans of any age or place should make to the reality

---

12. Genesis 8:21.

13. Genesis 2–3.

14. I.e., the fundamental demands of morality take on somewhat different forms in different cultures.

defined by the "Jewish-Christian" worldview; the "righteousness" of such laws, Deuteronomy believes, is self-evident to all.[15] Some demands in Deuteronomy, as Jews and Christians both concede, while expressing principles that are fundamental to the human condition, adapt those principles to the peculiar circumstances prevailing among those to whom "Torah" was first given.[16] Still other demands are in themselves arbitrary;[17] no rationale is given, for example, for the commanded exclusion of certain foods from Israelite diets.[18] Both the imposition of arbitrary divine demands and Israel's submission to them are justified, however, as fitting exhibits of the relationship between God and his people: even in deciding which food they should eat, God's people are not to pursue an independent path, but to delight in submission to the will of their benevolent Lord.

Jews use the term *Torah* for divine guidance, however it is given. A more technical usage employs the term to refer to the opening five books of the Hebrew Scriptures (the "books of Moses"). In Deuteronomy, the term refers to the divine stipulations that Israel undertook to observe when they entered a "covenant" with God. No peculiar goodness on Israel's part moved God to distinguish them with his favor.[19] But love them he did, and to make them "his" people, he liberated them from slavery to Pharaoh,[20] brought them "on eagles' wings" to Mount Sinai, and gave them laws by which they could demonstrate their adherence to his rule. As they do so, Deuteronomy never tires of intoning, they will prosper. Should they fail to do so, Deuteronomy never wearies of warning, they will perish. The choice is one of blessing or cursing, life or death.[21]

In a number of ways, God's "covenant" with Israel in Deuteronomy

---

15. Deuteronomy 4:5-8.

16. Some of these, indeed, now seem oppressive. Note, e.g., that the conditions of slaves are presupposed, though ameliorated, by the provisions of Deuteronomy 15:12-18.

17. So at least some representatives of the Jewish tradition have emphasized. With them we may reckon Paul. The argument of Romans 14 assumes that there is no inherent reason why certain foods should be forbidden or certain days observed as holy; yet Paul acknowledges that such observances can be a legitimate way to serve God.

18. Deuteronomy 14:3-21.

19. Deuteronomy 7:6-8; 9:4-6.

20. The story is told in Exodus 1–15.

21. Deuteronomy 11:26-28; 30:15-20.

provides a model of what, in the "Jewish-Christian" view, should be the relationship between God and his human creatures of all nations. Jews are thus meant to serve as a "light" to the peoples of the world.[22] God, as the source of good for all humankind, is the proper and worthy object of human devotion and trust. Israel's — and all humanity's — obedience is fitting not only because the Creator enjoys the prerogative to command his creatures but also because his requirements spell out the terms of their own well-being. But divine demands compel human decisions. It is not (from this perspective) for humans to decide what *is* good, thus imposing their own order and value on the world in which they live. In Deuteronomy, the good confronts Israel in the divine commands of Torah. For all humanity, in the "Jewish-Christian" view, the nature of the good is given in the already structured, already valued world of divine creation. The choice — for Israel and for all human beings — is whether they will *do* the good, thus aligning themselves with reality, or flout the good and live a lie, to their own inevitable destruction.

Deuteronomy stresses the starkness of the choice. God's demands, it insists, are neither complex nor difficult.[23] Yet Israel, the book repeatedly decries, seems constitutionally incapable of complying. This theme reaches its climax in chapter 32, the "Song of Moses." God's people are "perverse and crooked," "foolish and senseless."[24] They respond to God's goodness with a mulish and mutinous kick.[25] The chapter anticipates the detailing of Israel's recalcitrance in the books of Joshua, Judges, Samuel, and Kings, a story ending in divine judgment and exile.[26] Hope remains, however: if only Israel repents and returns to the Lord, he remains willing to deal mercifully with his people.[27] But for that to happen, Deuteronomy proposes, the divine Surgeon will need to "circumcise" Israel's "heart,"[28] cutting away its ingrained perversity.

---

22. For the notion, see Isaiah 43:10; 45:14; 60:2-3.

23. Deuteronomy 10:12-13; 30:11-14.

24. Deuteronomy 32:5-6.

25. Deuteronomy 32:15-18.

26. For other traditional statements of Israel's intractability, see Psalms 78 and 106, Ezekiel 20, and Nehemiah 9.

27. Deuteronomy 4:25-31; 30:1-5.

28. Deuteronomy 30:6.

. . . and in Paul

In the latter half of Romans 1, Paul denounced, without referring to divine law, the human revolt against reality: humans refuse to acknowledge God, defy the moral order of creation, engage in — and applaud — activities they know to be wrong. (That humans have moral sensibilities is presupposed in the observation that they defy them.)

Throughout chapter 2, a close relationship between human moral sensibilities and the Mosaic law is either stated or implied.[29] When Gentiles do what is right, they show (Paul believes) that, though they have no scroll of the law of God, its demand is "written on their hearts" and has left its imprint on their conscience.[30] Paul even allows that Gentiles may fulfill the law's commands better than Jews who have received its instruction: their conduct will add to the condemnation of unfaithful Jews.[31] Gentiles and Jews both are to be judged according to their works: well-doing will be rewarded, wickedness punished.[32] Paul insists on such judgment without any suggestion that "good" and "evil" have different content for Jews and Gentiles, though for the former, but not the latter, the terms are spelled out in the Mosaic code. Later in the letter Paul will claim that the demands of the law are "holy and just and good";[33] as in Deuteronomy 4:8, the primary point must be that the stipulations of the Mosaic code accurately reflect the appropriate demands of the reality within which all human beings — Jews and Gentiles alike — must live.[34]

In possessing the scrolls of the law, Jews are the recipients of a signal divine favor. On this point as well, Paul is at one with Deuteronomy. The Mosaic law may represent the mere spelling out of demands that apply to all people.[35] But the willful resistance of human beings to

29. References to "law" in this section of Romans usually refer to the Mosaic code (the metaphorical usage in Romans 2:14 is an obvious exception).

30. Romans 2:14-15.

31. Romans 2:27.

32. Romans 2:6-11.

33. Romans 7:12.

34. Paul ignores in these texts the more arbitrary demands of the law (e.g., the food laws) traditionally seen as binding only on Jews and enabling them further to express their adherence to the divine will.

35. The law is thus the "embodiment of knowledge and truth" (Romans 2:20).

the demands of the truth has left them "blind," "in darkness," "foolish," and in need of instruction. Guidance has been provided for Jews by the gift of Torah, a gift that enables them to enlighten others.[36]

Do they, however, first teach themselves?[37] After all, hearing the law is not the same as obeying it, and God can approve only the latter.[38] As in Deuteronomy, Israel's encounter with the divine demand compels a human decision; and Paul, like Deuteronomy 32 (a chapter he frequently cites) and the "Deuteronomistic History" of Joshua– 2 Kings, believes that Israel's recalcitrance is inveterate. It was right for God to remind his rebellious creatures of the demands of life in his world. It was, moreover, a great gift to Israel when they were entrusted with guidance of Torah's commands. But the response of human beings to divine law, in whatever form they encounter it, proves the same: they assert their independence by doing what is wrong. God's gift of the law has done nothing to alter this fundamental bent of the human will. The law's practical effect has been to indict, not remedy, human sinfulness.[39]

We note, in conclusion, three features of Paul's argument.

1. Paul allows that human beings (even Gentiles!) may do good,[40] yet he declares all humankind to be culpable before God.[41] His point is not that no one ever does things that are right, but rather that all people do things that are wrong. Indeed, the very selectivity with which humans sometimes choose to do the right, sometimes the wrong, may itself be seen as an expression of their setting themselves up as moral arbiters independent of God.[42]

2. Deuteronomy, like Proverbs, sees humans as experiencing the consequences of their choices during their lives on earth. Paul, in company with most Jews of his day, saw the effects of human deeds extending into the "world to come." Such an extension might seem to be demanded when the righteous appear to suffer and the wicked to prosper throughout their earthly sojourn: only in the afterlife can due recom-

---

36. Romans 2:17-20.
37. Romans 2:21-24.
38. Romans 2:13.
39. Romans 3:19-20.
40. Romans 2:7, 10, 14, and elsewhere.
41. Romans 3:19-20.
42. We will return to this issue in Chapter Eight below.

pense be given.[43] But the extension was also thought to be implicit in the commitment of an eternal God to a relationship with mortal human beings. The language of the Psalms at times invites the interpretation that death itself cannot terminate the human experience of joy in God's presence.[44] And surely (Jesus reasons in the Gospels), when God identified himself to Moses as the "God of Abraham, Isaac, and Jacob," he was not claiming to be the God of dead people: the relationship of an eternal God with those to whom he is committed *must* continue beyond their deaths.[45] But the extension of humanity's encounter with the Eternal into the "age to come" inevitably raises the stakes inherent in their choices.[46]

3. The Hebrew Scriptures constantly condemn Israel's waywardness, but they also summon Israel to repent. Does Paul not think that Israel *can* repent and do what is right? The answer, as later chapters in Romans clearly show, is No. Deuteronomy itself suggested that God would first need to "circumcise" Israel's heart.[47] Jeremiah, too, speaks of the need for God to change Israel's heart if they are to obey his commands.[48] And Ezekiel proposes a heart transplant as the necessary precondition.[49] Paul's point (to be developed in subsequent chapters) is similar. Human "flesh" refuses to bow itself to the divine will. To enlist humans on the side of the good, God must first transform humanity.

43. See Daniel 12:2.

44. Psalm 16:9-11; 73:23-26.

45. Matthew 22:31-32. Such is the "inner logic" with which Jews assimilated belief in life after death — whatever the "source" of the belief. The latter issue cannot be pursued here.

46. Romans 2:7-10.

47. Deuteronomy 30:6.

48. Jeremiah 31:33.

49. Ezekiel 36:26-27.

Chapter 5

The Divine Counter

ROMANS 3:21-31

SOME PEOPLE suffer severe pangs of guilt though they have incurred none, others incur monstrous guilt but betray no signs of disturbance. Why, and why not?

Consider (briefly — there are no profundities here) the following cases.

1. Those of us who have parked cars on side streets without noticing a "No Parking" sign are not inclined to feel any guilt about our action. Yet we pay a fine.

2. John feels guilty that he cheated his longtime friend and business partner. He is also, and not coincidentally, liable to prosecution.

3. Jim feels guilty for consuming, in a moment of weakness, food that he has been told he should not eat. The food is in fact harmless to his health.

4. June is distressed, believing that she has been a poor parent. Observers agree that she has done everything for her child that a parent can do.

The cases illustrate the following elementary distinction.

1. We *incur* guilt, whatever our feelings, when we violate a law or norm to which we are subject, as in cases one and two above.

2. We *feel* guilt when we believe that we have violated a law or norm that we believe to be both legitimate and significant, as in cases two, three, and four. Only in the second example above do incurred guilt and feelings of guilt overlap.

The modern West shows the same ambivalence about guilt as it does about the notion of wrongdoing. We can agree on the actual, objective guilt of those who break the laws of society or the rules of some institution or organization of which they are a part. But many are wary of limiting the freedom of individuals by suggesting that there are other — *moral* — norms by which they ought to govern their lives. Some, indeed, insist that there are no such norms, only conventions of particular societies. Others suspect the latter claims of overstatement but are themselves unable to articulate or to justify their belief in absolute moral standards. The result of our refusal to allow, or our inability to define and defend, universal norms is that feelings of guilt seem to lack warrant in all cases but those in which people transgress publicly acknowledged laws or rules. Pangs of guilt are frequently deemed irrational if not pathological.

Indeed, the laws of society themselves are apt to be construed as arbitrary and conventional when they are not thought to reflect "higher laws" of some sort. Clearly, lawbreakers are "guilty" in a technical, objective sense. But if the laws in force are perceived merely as sanctioned conventions designed to protect the interests and smooth the functioning of society, and if, in other areas, we lionize individual freedom, we should not be surprised when independently minded individuals wonder why they need to submit to the conventions we call "laws" and feel no guilt when they flout them. Who says, after all, that the law should not be broken? Society? Why should anyone listen to "society"? Because it has the power to punish? What if I believe I can escape punishment? Without other resources to supplement it, the rhetoric of individual freedom seems incapable of devising an answer.

Yet many of us are distressed by the brazen absence of any sense of guilt shown by some who commit heinous crimes. We are appalled when people who cheat and swindle, who grossly neglect or abuse their dependents, who murder for the pocket-change of their victims, appear to regret only that they were caught. They *ought* to feel guilty, we protest — though our uncertainty about the status or force of moral claims leaves us ill equipped to justify the burden of guilt we fain would assign them.

Such a dilemma is surely a characteristic product of the perspectives and peculiar emphases of the modern West. Paul would have been as hard pressed to see the point of our dilemma as we are to understand his language of atonement. In this chapter we will begin with a modern *approximation* of biblical notions of guilt and atonement, proceed with a few features of their occurrence in the Hebrew Scriptures, then conclude with a few observations on Paul.

Of Guilt and Atonement

Guilt ensues from the violation of valid norms. And one "norm" whose validity most of us would recognize requires that those who benefit from the kindness of others respond with some gesture of reciprocation. "You could at least have said thank you!" is a reproach that we often think justified, though significant benefits, bestowed at considerable sacrifice on the part of the donor, may well oblige us beyond a mere expression of thanks. Those who accept the benefits given by others but withhold any gesture of reciprocation would seem to have incurred an outstanding "debt." To take a different tack, the positive harm we admittedly do to others would seem to bring us guilt and call for compensation. (I am not the only parent who, having shouted unnecessarily at a son, has attempted to "make it up" to him with an apology and a trip to a donut shop — the latter receiving much the better hearing.) If compensation of some kind is not forthcoming, the metaphor of "unpaid debt" again seems warranted. In short, it seems impossible that we could coexist with others without constantly incurring "debts" — of one kind or another — to them, and they to us.

We can, of course, simply ignore such claims, but we are not, it would seem, "playing fair" if we do so. Those we harm are *due* some reparation; benefactors are *due* at least some token of compensation. We may see these "norms" as inherent in the human condition apart from any mention of the supernatural. If, however, we allow that we owe our life, our world, and "every good and perfect gift" to the bounty of the Creator, then it is easy to conceive a (largely undischarged) human "debt" to God. We have scarcely given God due recognition for his favors. If, moreover, other human beings are his creatures, then our debt to God increases with each wrong we do to them. Furthermore, assuming that, if we ourselves are the handiwork of a wise and benevolent Creator, such a Creator must have intended something more (and rather different) to be made of our own lives than sober introspection will allow that we have achieved, our guilt toward God must include our distorted goals and sullied ideals. In short, a monstrous "debt" to God is much more easily conceived than the means by which any human might be thought to discharge it.

The "debt," on this understanding of the human condition, cannot simply be ignored: that would be to deprive of significance the most basic truths about the human presence in God's world. On the other hand, it is, presumably, a divine prerogative to spell out the required compensation. But Jewish and Christian tradition goes further. Convinced as it is of the divine goodwill toward humankind, it declares that God himself has made available the means for humans to discharge their "debt" to him. To have their indebtedness absolved, their guilt toward God removed, they need only avail themselves of the divine provision. Conversely, to refuse such a response is necessarily to retain one's "indebtedness" — indeed, to compound it with contempt for the goodness of God.

An Added Dimension

Along some such lines we may approximate biblical notions of guilt and atonement. To enter more fully into the latter field of vision, we need not discount anything of what has been said. We will, however, need to add a further dimension.

For us, the nonhuman world serves as the neutral scene of human moral (and other) activities. A crime committed may or may not be detected by relevant authorities. If they detect it, they may or may not choose to prosecute. If they prosecute, they may or may not choose to punish. In any case, the punishment to be assigned must be determined by a competent judge. Undetected, unprosecuted, or unpunished crimes are commonly thought to bear no consequences.

That the biblical view is another follows necessarily from the conviction that the ultimate Judge of all is both all-seeing and unflinching in his determination to root out evil from his creation; but it follows as well from the integration of human beings within the created order. The drama of human morality implicates more than God and humankind. Nature itself is "charged" with divine goodness. Its natural course is both a testimony to and a celebration of God's faithfulness to his creation. In such a world, human self-absorption is an unwelcome intrusion, a violation and contamination of what was innocent and good. Inevitably, nature itself is disrupted when humans flout its order. Thus, the earth that witnessed Adam's declaration of independence thereafter bore him thorns and thistles.[1] Having swallowed Abel's blood, it yielded no fruit for his murderer.[2] A land defiled by pagan abominations "spewed out" its inhabitants.[3] Famine decimated the land when the king failed to observe an oath.[4]

A telling reflection of the difference between the biblical perspective and our own is the use in Hebrew of a single word where we require two for "misdeed" and "punishment." On learning that the earth that has received his brother's blood will never provide him a refuge, Cain declares (literally) that his "iniquity" (note well: not, in Hebrew, a distinct word for "punishment") is more than he can bear.[5] If Israelites renege on a solemn commitment, they can be sure that their "sin" (note again: not an arbitrarily affixed "punishment") will "find [them] out."[6] In a neutral, purely material universe, the only negative consequence of our misdeeds is the "punishment" we are assigned; and since punishment does not follow every crime and its imposition is at the (somewhat arbitrary) discretion of a different party, a verbal distinction between "crime" and "punishment" is required. In the divinely charged nature of biblical horizons, however, wrongdoing is perceived as a disturbance of the good that cannot but have evil consequences. The initial act and the bane of sin are two stages in a single process, appropriately given a single designate: "sin" (or "iniquity"). It is thus not so much the harshness of an arbitrarily imposed "punishment" that Cain laments, but his own "iniquity," the enormity of whose bane he had not anticipated. Even when the Hebrew law-codes spell out what should be done to wrongdoers, the underlying notion is the same: wrongdoing brings disaster. The administration of justice merely assures that the wrongdoers themselves are the ones who experience its brunt. They are thus made to

1. Genesis 3:17-18.
2. Genesis 4:11-12.
3. Leviticus 18:26-28.
4. 2 Samuel 21:1.
5. Genesis 4:13.
6. Numbers 32:23.

"bear their iniquity";[7] by another graphic turn of phrase, their sin is said to be brought down upon their own "heads."[8]

If, then, a benevolent deity wishes to deliver humans from the bane of their guilt, he cannot simply overlook their misdeeds. The latter option would be excluded in any case by the divine *tzedakah,* God's unswerving faithfulness in upholding (or restoring) the goodness of his creation: divine goodness cannot be indifferent to evil. But, beyond that necessity of the Lord's "righteousness," divine disregard for sin would do nothing to interrupt the fatal link between its two stages. The incursion of sin must be countered, its contamination expunged. The divine solution is cultic "atonement": God designates a sacrificial animal as the substitute victim on whom the bane of human sin can be channeled and exhausted. This remedy avoids any suggestion that God overlooks the distinction between good and evil, thereby condoning sin. At the same time it provides for humans deliverance from the consequences of their iniquities. All that is required on their side is faithful participation in the divinely instituted ceremonies of atonement. They thus make their own the divine provision for their absolution.[9]

The preceding summary is, of course, too simple, straightforward, and even mechanical to do justice to reality as the ancient Israelites themselves conceived it. They were abundantly aware that human relationships are so interwoven that many people suffer the bane of sins for which they bear no personal responsibility.[10] And no doubt it was largely when nature posed an *extraordinary* threat to human well-being that specific acts of wrongdoing were sought out as the cause. Nonetheless, the following convictions seem both basic and common within biblical horizons.

1. Humans sin — even the best of them.
2. Sin brings bane upon human affairs.
3. Nature suffers as well.[11]

7. Leviticus 17:16.
8. 1 Kings 2:33; 8:32.
9. See Leviticus 4:1–6:7; 16:1-34.
10. See Exodus 20:5; 2 Samuel 24:17.
11. Note Paul's claim in Romans 8:19-23 that God has consigned creation to the suffering of decay and futility as long as humans bear the marks of sin. Note, too, the famous vision in Isaiah 11:1-9 of a restored and peaceful nature accompanying the rule of righteousness over the nations.

4. Sin must be atoned for if its bane is to be broken.
5. God, in his continued goodness toward his sinful creatures, provides for the atonement of their sins.

Early Christian Perspectives

The language of cultic atonement used in the Hebrew Scriptures was taken over by the early Christians when they spoke of Jesus' death.[12] The adoption of the terminology was inevitably accompanied by a devaluation of the significance of Israel's rites of atonement. The early Christians did not need to deny that the latter had been divinely instituted; but they could hardly see them as effecting a genuine atonement for sin[13] or, at any rate, as atoning for the sins of non-Israelite humanity. A common alternative was to see them as preparatory, pedagogic devices: Israel's repeated sacrifices highlighted the crisis provoked by human sin, the divine willingness to forgive, and the necessity of an atoning sacrifice. In this way, though themselves far from a match for the sins of the world, Israel's rites foreshadowed the once-for-all, universally effective self-sacrifice of God's son.[14] *They* were symbolic; *he* is the "[true] place [or means] of expiation" for the sin of all humankind.[15]

Paul's reference to atonement in our passage is rightly regarded as traditional, a reaffirmation of central Christian convictions. Five features of the Pauline restatement call for comment here.

1. Over the centuries atonement has often been portrayed as the ingenious means by which two opposing divine characteristics can both find satisfactory expression. Divine *holiness* (or "righteousness") requires punishment for sin, whereas divine *mercy* requires that God save

12. An important intermediary step, much exploited by the early Christians, was provided by Isaiah 53, in which the prophet speaks of a *human* "offering for sin" (verse 10), of a man upon whom "the Lord laid the iniquity of us all" (verse 6; note also the language of verses 5, 8, 11, and 12).

13. Note, e.g., Hebrews 10:4: "It is impossible that the blood of bulls and goats should take away sin."

14. See Hebrews 10:1-14; and note the language of 1 Corinthians 5:7 and Colossians 2:16-17. I will discuss the notion of divine "sonship" in Chapter Seven.

15. Romans 3:25; see John 1:29; 1 John 2:2.

the sinner. The death of Christ, as a divinely provided substitute for the death deserved by sinners, is seen as allowing both of these divine attributes their proper function.

Such an interpretation, in spite of its venerable pedigree, cannot claim Paul as its progenitor. For Paul, the death of Christ represents, not the resolution of a tension within the deity, but the solution to a human dilemma achieved by God's *tzedakah*,[16] his faithfulness in upholding creation's goodness. It is divine *tzedakah* that in Christ's death refuses to blur the distinction between good and evil by ignoring or trivializing the latter: How *could* God demonstrate more clearly the wrongfulness and the dread disruption of human sin than by giving his son's life as its atonement? But the same divine *tzedakah*, the same divine commitment to the goodness of his creation, is operative in the death of Christ to restore sinful humanity to its intended place in creation's order. In short, the message of Romans 3:21-26 is not that mercy triumphs over judgment, but that, in a world gone awry, divine goodness has reasserted itself, granting drastic recognition to the reality of sin, yet restoring what sin had disfigured to a place of glory in God's creation.

2. Those who know their sins to be atoned for, and themselves restored to divine favor, are labeled (to use Paul's Greek term) *dikaioume-noi*; that is, they are the beneficiaries of God's *dikaiosynē* (Greek) or *tzedakah* (Hebrew). The standard English rendering, "justified," is at best the least inadequate translation. The point, in any case, is not that such people are, by a divine legal fiction, "declared righteous" though in fact they remain sinners, nor that they have suddenly been transformed from sinners into right-behaving individuals, but simply that their sin with its bane has been atoned for and they are thus, by God's goodness, once again in good standing with their Creator and Judge.

3. Paul's concern here is not with human feelings of guilt, but with God's overcoming and expunging of the (objective) guilt incurred by human sin. There are, no doubt, psychological benefits for those who know themselves to be guilty of sundry sins but who believe that God loves, forgives, and accepts them for the sake of Christ. Indeed, something of the kind may have been in Paul's mind when (on one reading

---

16. Paul uses the Greek word *dikaiosynē*, in his day a time-honored equivalent for the Hebrew term.

of the text) he invites his readers in Romans 5:1 to "enjoy [their] peace with God." But the drama of sin and atonement in Romans 3 has all creation as its stage, not just the human psyche.

4. The divine "redemption" (or "costly liberation") is made available in Christ Jesus to Jews and non-Jews alike. It is thus a reassertion of divine goodness toward, and sovereignty over, all humankind.[17] Jews were given the scrolls of the law, Gentiles were not. But humans of every race have sinned and relinquished their place in God's created order. The law drew attention to human rebellion against God's goodness but could not quell the rebellion. Now God's *tzedakah* has been demonstrated "apart from the law"[18] and made available, on identical terms, to Jews and Gentiles alike. God (as Paul insists that his gospel shows) is God of the Jews — and God of the Gentiles also.[19]

5. The requisite human response is that of "faith." This latter topic is crucial and will occupy us in the next chapter, as it does Paul in Romans 4. It is sufficient to note for the moment that the required response does nothing, in Paul's mind, to jeopardize the nature of divine redemption as a gift bestowed freely upon sinners by the grace of God.[20]

17. Romans 3:22-24, 29-30.
18. Romans 3:21.
19. Romans 3:29.
20. Romans 3:24.

Chapter 6

Faith's Awakening

ROMANS 4:1-25

IN THIS CHAPTER we will consider faith: its character, its model, and its place in Paul's thought.

Love's Awakening — and Faith

In an earlier chapter, Barb and Bob were singled out, perhaps unduly, for an honored place in the narrative. It is time I told of Tammy and Tom.

The mutual "discovery" of Barb and Bob, you may recall, was quite unexpected. Indeed, had they been on the "lookout," Barb never would have dreamed of looking in Bob's direction, nor Bob in Barb's: they had known each other — and taken each other for granted — too long for that. Each thought decently enough of the other. But they did so seldom. And *never* in romantic terms. Until, that is, they found themselves together one afternoon discussing some trivial incident that had taken place in their town . . . and their eyes were opened and the world changed forever its accustomed hue.

The story of Tammy and Tom is a little different. Tom, feeling isolated by the strange change that had come over Bob and a score of his other friends, had begun a search in earnest for *his* "Barb." Likewise, Tammy noticed a change in Barb. More significant in her case, however, was the knowledge she had acquired — having absorbed a thousand movies and skimmed a good half-dozen books — of precisely how things were supposed to happen for a girl of her age and practiced charms. As a result, she was eagerly awaiting the appearance of someone (the hackneyed phrase "the right person" is here perhaps overly specific) with whom they could happen. And there was *Tom!* And *there* was Tammy!

What chiefly appealed to Tammy and Tom about Tom and Tammy, apart from their unmistakable availability, was the evident interest each of them had in being half of a "Tammy and Tom." They played their parts with the consummate ease of those who had re-hearsed every line and gesture in a thousand wakeful dreams. Full attention was required only to see that the proper proper names ("O Tom! Tom!" "Yes, Tammy!") were inserted at crucial junctures; and — rest assured, anxious Reader! — they were equal to the task, though their preoccupation with their own part would no doubt have blinded them in any case to the slips of their fellow actor. Charitably inclined as we are — and having once been young ourselves — we will leave them with the wish that when, in the course of the next several months, they actually begin the process of discovering each other, they will like what they see.

For Barb and Bob's experience we felt justified in dusting off a well-worn tag: they had "fallen in love" with each other. Of Tammy and Tom, the most we can say is that they were "in love" with the idea of "falling in love." Apart from his availability, Tom's character played very little role in shaping Tammy's experience of their relationship, at least in its initial stages; nor did Tammy's personality figure largely in Tom's perturbation. Had Tammy's Tom been Tim, or Tom's Tammy a Tina, they would scarcely have noticed the difference.

The contrast with Barb and Bob is again marked. No doubt they exaggerate each other's perfections. But Bob's whole world, when he is with her and when he is not, is unquestionably focused on Barb: *her* smile, *her* voice, *her* eyes, *her* wit, *her* gait, *her* love. And Barb's thoughts are overwhelmed with Bob's *Bob*-ness. Suggest not to them that Barb could be Brenda, or Bob, Bill! There is, Bob would insist, nothing wrong with Brenda: but she is not *Barb*. Nor, in Barb's beholding, is Bill, Bob. Should it ever happen (the suggestion, for the moment, is heretical) that Barb and Bob have a falling out, and Barb should "fall in love" with Bill and Bob with Brenda, they will feel even then — and quite rightly — that neither "Barb and Bill" nor "Brenda and Bob" is the same thing as "Barb and Bob." The experience of falling in love *with someone* is inevitably as unique as are the personalities of those involved.

In short, love of a person is neither oblivious nor indifferent to the unique nature of the person loved. We may appropriately speak of our *love* for different people (a grandparent and an aunt, a parent and a child, a spouse and a friend), and even for pets. We are saying that we care deeply for them all, that we are committed to their well-being. Still, our love for each is elicited, experienced, and expressed in ways peculiar to each relationship. Love is impossible without an object, and the nature of love's object colors the nature of the love.

The same is true of faith.[1] "Faith" (or "trust") can hardly be spoken of in an absolute sense: one trusts *someone* (or *something*) one has found, or has reason to believe, trust*worthy*. In requiring an object, then, "trust" is like love; and it, too, is elicited, experienced, and expressed in ways dependent upon its object. One *may* "trust" an exceptional politician, but not in quite the same way one "trusts" a parent, or a spouse, or a friend — or God.

Now one can decide to act as *though* one trusted someone, much as Tammy and Tom acted the parts of those who had fallen in love with each other. But the trust of mature human beings, like (Barb and Bob's) love, is not a unilateral decision indifferent to the character of its object, but a response elicited by a perception of the trustworthiness or goodness of the one trusted; and the strength and character of our trust are inevitably dependent upon our perception of the character of the one we trust. Ask those who have "fallen in love" why they have done so, and they are likely to respond, not in terms of their own decision-making process (they will hardly allow that they "decided" to fall in love!), but simply with what they find "lovable" about the object of their devotion. Ask those who "trust" why they do so, and their answer will indicate what they find worthy of trust in the object of their faith.

---

1. The Greek word *pistis* is used both for "faith, trust, confidence" and for "faithfulness, loyalty, reliability." In the corpus of his extant writings, Paul has occasion to use the word in both senses. Our immediate concern, however, is with the former usage.

Faith and Father Abraham

Paul cites Abraham (he is called first "Abram," then "Abraham" in the Genesis account) as the "father" of all who believe.[2] We must give some consideration to Abraham if we are to understand Paul.

Abraham's story begins in earnest in Genesis 12 with a striking divine commission.

> The Lord said to Abram, "Set forth from your land, your kinsfolk, and your father's household, for a land that I will show you. And I will make of you a great nation. I will bless you and make your name great, and you will become a standard of blessing. I will bless those who bless you and curse those who curse you. All the earth's clans, when they bless themselves, will use you as the standard of blessing" [or, "All the earth's clans will be blessed in you"].[3]

The laconic narrative continues, "And Abram set forth as the Lord had told him";[4] and we may well see his behavior at the outset as a model of obedience to God. Still, his obedience was clearly preceded and motivated by an equally exemplary *trust:* Abram sets out for a yet undisclosed destination on the verbal assurance that (1) it will be shown to him; (2) he will (there) become the founder of a great nation and (3) be abundantly "blessed" (4) to the point that his name will be used proverbially of one divinely favored. The promises are incredible; yet, if Abram is to act upon them, he must give them credence. Abram necessarily *trusted* God when he obeyed him as he did.

Abram's obedience is somewhat spotty in the stories that follow: it lags where his faith flags. Twice he calls his wife Sarah his sister, lying out of fear for his life — though God's yet unfulfilled promises require his survival.[5] In Genesis 16, Abram (at his wife's prompting) decides that the divine initiative requires human assistance if it is ever to come to fruition. On the other hand, when his prayer of despair is met, not with divine action, but with a still more incredible restatement of the

2. Romans 4:11-12; also Galatians 3:7.
3. Genesis 12:1-3.
4. Genesis 12:4.
5. Genesis 12:10-20; 20:1-18.

initial divine promise, Abram, we are told, "believed God; and God credited it to him as righteousness."[6] And Abraham's faith passes a still more stupefying test when he trusts God though the latter commands the sacrifice of his son.[7]

Scripture portrays Abraham as God's intimate "friend," one who "walked" in God's presence, "stood" before him, was kept apprised of divine plans — and even allowed a part in their formation.[8] Such a relationship bred and reflected the trust for which Abraham serves as a Pauline model.

The Place of Faith in Paul

That God is worthy of trust is an inevitable consequence of the "Jewish-Christian" vision.[9] So, too, is that humans, in choosing an independent course for themselves rather than responding to divine goodness as they ought, signal their distrust in God. But if we grant the truth of Paul's gospel of divine redemption, then what God has done in Christ has been (among other things) to furnish a fresh and prodigious demonstration that he is worthy of human trust: so great has been his commitment to restoring the goodness of creation, and so strong has been his love for humankind, that he himself has provided a costly atonement for the sins of those who have wronged him. The natural, appropriate response evoked by the proclamation of the Christian message should thus be faith, or trust, in God: faith is awakened by hearing the word of Christ.[10]

A few observations are in order.

1. Paul can speak both of "trusting" or "believing in" God[11] and of "believing *that* God raised [Christ] from the dead."[12] These two

---

6. Genesis 15:2-6.

7. Genesis 22:1-14. The narrative goes on to say that in the end the sacrifice was not required.

8. Isaiah 41:8; Genesis 17:1; 18:17-33.

9. For the sense in which I use the phrase, see Chapter One, n. 7.

10. See Romans 10:17.

11. Romans 4:3, 5; 10:11. The Greek verb is *pisteuō*, related to the noun *pistis*, "faith" or "trust."

12. Romans 10:9.

types of faith ([i] confidence in a person and [ii] the conviction that a particular claim is true) are not as distinct as they are sometimes made out to be. Humans (according to the "Jewish-Christian" vision) should trust God, but do not. They learn once again what it is to trust him (type [i] above) when they take seriously (or *believe*) the content of some claim demonstrating his trustworthiness (type [ii] above). A fine example is offered by Exodus 14:31: Israel's faith *in God* (and in Moses his servant) was kindled by their seeing (and believing!) that he had delivered them from the Egyptians. Similarly, for Paul, a proper trust in God is awakened with the belief that he has acted on our behalf in Christ: "We are those who trust in [God] who raised Jesus our Lord from the dead, who was handed over for our transgressions and raised that we might be restored to God's favor."[13] Appropriate faith in God thus accompanies the conviction that the Christian message of what he has done is true.[14]

2. God's demonstration of his trustworthiness in Christ is thus the means not merely of atoning for human sins but also of spurring rebellious humans to a living faith in God. On the other hand, the proclamation of Christ's death as the atonement for human sin cannot benefit those who do not respond in faith. By continuing to act like gods in their own world rather than trust God in his, they persist in the very lie that breeds the sins for which Christ died.

3. Although faith in the God who has demonstrated his love for humans in Christ is an inevitable *requirement* of the gospel, it is not, for Paul, an achievement of the believer. He distinguishes between the compensation people receive for work they do and the "righteousness" (that is, the restoration to divine favor brought about by divine *tzedakah*)[15] experienced by believers as a gift of divine grace.[16] Such "righteousness" is seen as a gift[17] in part because those so favored were themselves "ungodly," "sinners," "enemies" of God,[18] and it is only what

13. Romans 4:24-25.

14. 1 Peter 1:21 provides a good summary of this point: "*by Christ* you believe *in God* who raised him from the dead and gave him glory, *so that your faith and hope might be in God.*"

15. On the term, see Chapter Two above.

16. Romans 4:3-5.

17. Note Romans 5:17.

18. Romans 4:5; 5:6, 8, 10.

God has done in Christ that has atoned for their sins; and in part because their faith in God is itself not a product of their own initiative, but a response evoked by the news of God's staggering demonstration of goodness.[19]

4. On the other hand, Paul's well-known contrast between "faith" and "works," and his insistence that only the former is required for "justification," must not be misconstrued as an endorsement of mere belief that is not accompanied and expressed by appropriate behavior. The following observations (each expanded upon elsewhere) are crucial to our understanding of his point.

i. The law of Moses required that adherents of God's covenant with Israel submit to its provisions if they were to maintain their position of favor as God's people. Paul insists that that covenant has now given way to a new covenant requiring faith in Christ.[20] One must not impose the provisions (or "works") of the (old) Mosaic law (such as circumcision or the dietary laws) on those who belong to God's (new) people through faith.[21]

ii. The giving of the Mosaic law was accompanied by dual sanctions: blessing and life for those who observed it, a curse and death for those who did not.[22] Yet, given humanity's resistance to the divine will and insistence upon its own independent path (paradigmatically demonstrated in Israel's notoriously "hard hearts" and "stiff necks"), the law's only operative sanction, Paul believes, was that of cursing and death;[23] and the covenant to which the law belonged can be summed up as one of "condemnation" and "death."[24] Thus, even in the period of the law's validity, its subjects did not enjoy divine favor because they faithfully observed its "works." Rather, the law served to indict human sin.[25]

iii. Those who belong to God's people through faith in Christ could not, in their prior state of rebellion against God, show behavior pleasing to God. They must first abandon their rebellion and submit to God in

---

19. Romans 10:17.
20. 2 Corinthians 3:6-14; see also Galatians 4:21–5:1.
21. See Galatians 2:11-21.
22. Deuteronomy 11:26-28; 30:15-20.
23. Romans 7:9-11; 8:2, 6-8; Galatians 3:10.
24. 2 Corinthians 3:6-7, 9.
25. Romans 3:19-20.

faith. This transformation of "ungodly" people was not brought about by a unilateral decision on the part of the "ungodly," but through the proclamation of God's salvation. In this respect, the prior necessity of the divine summons to faith is like God's "calling" of Isaac and Jacob to be forefathers of Israel: a "calling" motivated, again, not by the "works" of those called, but only by the grace of the divine Caller.[26]

iv. On the other hand, Paul is adamant that faith in God must express itself[27] in appropriate behavior: in this sense "works" are demanded of the Christian.[28] In his mind, however, such works are distinct from those he proscribes (or declares ineffective) in that the former are the products neither of adherence to an obsolete covenant nor of the strivings of rebels against God. They are rather expressions of a life of faith initiated and empowered (as we shall see in subsequent chapters) by divine grace.[29]

5. Paul can speak as though "faith" began with the coming of Christ,[30] a claim that seems consistent with the view that humanity, apart from Christ, is in a state of rebellion against God. On the other hand, he does allow Abraham as a model of Christian faith: a common pattern is seen in that Abraham, like the Christian, was "justified" (that is, he enjoyed God's favor) not because of "works," but because he responded with faith to an initiative of God's grace.[31]

6. Paul stresses once again in Romans 4 that the same path of faith is open to Jews and non-Jews alike. Abraham serves as the model and

26. See Romans 9:10-12; 11:5-6.

27. Note, e.g., the phrase "obedience of faith" in Romans 1:5. What "counts," according to Galatians 5:6, is "faith that is active in love."

28. See Romans 8:13; 2 Corinthians 5:10.

29. 1 Corinthians 15:9-10; 2 Corinthians 12:9-10; Romans 8:13-14; Galatians 5:16-25.

30. Galatians 3:23, 25.

31. Romans 4:3-5, 17-22. Galatians 3:8 can be construed as saying that Abraham himself was a believer in the Christian gospel inasmuch as it was implicit in the divine promises given him. Such a reading would corroborate the claim that faith is necessarily linked to the coming of Christ, even among those who lived before his appearing. Paul does not, in any case, believe that all who lived prior to Christ are simply condemned. Without elaborating the point, he speaks of the time prior to Christ's death as one of temporary divine "forbearance." That sins were then temporarily "passed over," not condoned, is demonstrated by the event that brought the period of forbearance to an end: the atoning death of Christ (Romans 3:25-26).

"father" of all who believe, not only of circumcised Jews but also of uncircumcised Gentiles: he himself believed, and was declared righteous, while he was still uncircumcised.[32] Nor (Paul goes on to argue) does the subsequent giving of the law limit the blessing of Abraham to the law's recipients. Such an inference would set aside faith as the criterion of blessing,[33] misconstrue the actual effect of the law (which was to pronounce judgment on its transgressors),[34] and limit the efficacy of what God promised Abraham to the nation to whom the law was given — contrary to the very terms of the initial commitment ("I have made you a father of many nations").[35] The story of Abraham, Paul concludes, has been recorded for the benefit of all who believe in, and are "justified" by, the God who raised Jesus from the dead.[36]

32. Romans 4:9-12.
33. Romans 4:13-14.
34. Romans 4:15.
35. Romans 4:16-17.
36. Romans 4:23-25.

Chapter 7

Just Cause for Joy

ROMANS 5:1-11

THE PERCEPTION of God's goodness to humankind in Christ, Paul believes, properly elicits trust. It also, he assures us, evokes joy.

Of Goodness and Joy

No doubt the closest analogy to what he means is, again, provided by the experience of human love that is enthralled with its beloved and, at the same time, has come to view the world itself as home to a goodness and beauty it had not hitherto known existed. With the discovery comes joy: a profound sense of the goodness of life in which one is accepted, welcomed, even loved by the "other" who matters most in all the world.

The psalmists of the Bible found joy in the presence of God: an overwhelming sense that, wherever one found oneself,[1] and whatever one's circumstances, God is there — and God is good.[2] The joy may be expressed, as the psalms frequently enjoin, with music and dance and boisterous shouts. It may find voice in a quiet prayer of assurance: "When I awake, I am still with thee."[3] In any case, the psalmists re-

---

1. So at least Psalm 139.
2. See the discussion of the Psalms in Chapter Two above.
3. Psalm 139:18, King James Version.

peatedly speak of discovering in the Eternal not only their provision
and protection but also their heart's delight.

> Thou hast put gladness in my heart,
>   more than in the time
>   that their corn and their wine increased.[4]

> In thy presence is fulness of joy;
>   at thy right hand
>   there are pleasures for evermore.[5]

> Delight thyself also in the Lord;
>   and he shall give thee
>   the desires of thine heart.[6]

Not incidental to the pleasure was the belief that its enjoyment was
mutual.

> He delighteth not in the strength of the horse;
>   he taketh not pleasure in the legs of a man.
> The Lord taketh pleasure in them that fear him,
>   in those that hope in his mercy.[7]

The psalmists' joy is rooted in their conviction that, circumstances
notwithstanding, life is good and that they have a share in its goodness,
loved by the One who matters most. Praise, for them, is the natural,
appropriate venting of joy: to praise the Lord is "fitting" and "good."[8]

For his part, Paul believes (as we have seen) that a spirit of rebellion
has infected all humankind, and done so to disastrous effect; but also
that God has reasserted his *tzedakah*,[9] provided atonement for the rav-
ages of sin, and in the process summoned humanity to return to the
embrace of his goodness. To trust the God who has demonstrated his

---

4. Psalm 4:7, King James Version.
5. Psalm 16:11, King James Version.
6. Psalm 37:4, King James Version.
7. Psalm 147:10-11, King James Version.
8. Psalm 92:1; 147:1.
9. For the term, see Chapter Two above.

love in Christ is to be "reconciled" to him, to be "at peace" with him and restored to his good graces, and, at the same time, to be assured of a share in God's eternal glory:[10] cause enough, Paul declares, for exuberant celebration.[11]

This celebration can continue whatever one's outward circumstances: the latter cannot imperil one's place in the divine favor.[12] Paul provides several grounds for persistent joy.

First, even hard times serve a good purpose, strengthening and proving the mettle of those who endure them and sharpening their hope for deliverance from distresses that are inevitable to life in a creation marred by sin.[13]

Second, the hope of Christians will not disappoint them: of this they can rest assured in spite of present afflictions because they know already the reality of God's love in their heart. That knowledge has been conveyed by the "holy spirit who has been given" to them.[14]

A brief digression is in order here.

Joy and the Spirit

The Hebrew Scriptures contain a number of accounts in which the divine spirit is said to come upon individuals, provoking at times eccentric behavior,[15] but also enabling them to perform feats beyond their normal capacities. A gift for prophecy[16] and the performance of extraordinary exploits in battle[17] are frequently attributed to the onrush of God's spirit, though the presence of the latter could be seen in more temperate endowments as well.[18] Not surprisingly, an ideal took shape that envisioned the day when all God's people would

10. Romans 5:1-2, 10.
11. Romans 5:11.
12. Romans 5:3.
13. Romans 5:2-4; see also Romans 8:18-39.
14. Romans 5:5.
15. See, e.g., 1 Samuel 19:20-24.
16. Numbers 11:25-26.
17. Judges 3:10.
18. Exodus 35:30-35.

possess his spirit.[19] *All* would then prophesy. And perhaps, as Ezekiel ventured to forecast, God's people, in possession of God's spirit, might even prove able, in spite of their wayward past, to obey God's laws.[20]

The beginnings of the Christian movement were accompanied by charismatic outbreaks interpreted as evidence that this prophetic vision had found fulfillment: God's spirit had been poured out upon God's people.[21] This conviction was central to Paul's Christian thought. The presence of the spirit represented for him a kind of anticipatory gift, a first installment or guarantee of the full glory still in store for believers.[22] It empowered Christian ethical behavior[23] and equipped individual believers to make their own distinctive contribution to the well-being of the community.[24]

But the divine spirit given to believers was also seen (and this is the point in the passage under consideration) as the source of their experience of the divine Presence, both in their community gatherings[25] and in their private devotion. In times of weakness (Paul writes in Romans 8), believers sense the help of the spirit, bearing their prayers into the presence of God with sighs too deep for words.[26] The same spirit's testimony in their hearts gives believers treasured assurance of their acceptance as God's children.[27] According to our passage, the reality of God's love is conveyed by the indwelling spirit to the hearts of believers, a communication Paul believes so telling and unmistakable that it grounds an unwavering conviction of bliss to come.

Paul can speak in one breath of the spirit as being that of God, in another as that of Christ:[28] the character of the divine presence sensed by believers is the loving character of the God whom they know through Christ. At the same time, Paul regularly distinguishes between God and

19. Numbers 11:29; Joel 2:28-29.

20. Ezekiel 36:27.

21. Acts 2:1-18; 1 Corinthians 12:7-11.

22. Romans 8:23; 2 Corinthians 1:22.

23. Romans 7:6; 8:4; Galatians 5:16-25. Note the parallel to Ezekiel's forecast mentioned above.

24. 1 Corinthians 12:4-11.

25. Note the reference to the "communion of the holy spirit" in 2 Corinthians 13:14.

26. Romans 8:26.

27. Romans 8:14-16; also Galatians 4:6.

28. See, e.g., Romans 8:9, 14.

the spirit[29] and between Christ and the spirit.[30] Indeed, there are trinitarian formulations in Paul, most famously that invoking the blessing of the "Lord Jesus Christ," "God," and the "holy spirit" on the Corinthian believers in 2 Corinthians 13:14.[31]

The church of a later day, when defining, communicating, and defending its faith, felt constrained to insist that the "one God" (or the God who was one in "substance" or "essence") was existent in "three persons" (so they expressed the distinction within the deity required by the Christian revelation of a God who had acted in Christ and was now present in the Holy Spirit). That Paul himself neither had nor felt the need of such ready formulas is self-evident. We may nonetheless grant that the later church was striving to find formulations that did justice to features present in the Pauline texts (or, better, to the Reality that they believed underlay them).

*   *   *

For Paul, further proof of God's enduring love for believers is found in that its greatest demonstration was given when they were at their very worst: when they were still "weak," "ungodly," "sinners," God's "enemies." His love did not abandon them then; it is unthinkable that it should do so now when they have been "reconciled" to God and enjoy his favor.[32]

The greatest proof of God's love, however, was the death, for sinners, of God's "son."[33] The introduction of the latter term warrants another digression.

The Proof of Divine Love — and the Divine "Son"

According to biblical tradition, the first monarch to rule over the united Israelite tribes was Saul: tall of stature, short in counsel, moody, suspi-

---

29. The spirit, as noted above, is said to convey to God the prayers of believers (Romans 8:26).

30. Note, e.g., the distinction in Romans 8:11.

31. See also Romans 8:3-4; and (with remarkable compactness) Galatians 4:6.

32. Romans 5:6-11.

33. Romans 5:10.

cious, increasingly isolated, ultimately abandoned by God to his foes.[34] He was succeeded, not by his son, but by David, a court musician and, of course, the original Giant-Killer. To David, the prophet Nathan declared that God would establish his dynasty forever and be a father to his son, never abandoning him as he had abandoned Saul.[35] The oracle was the subject of several psalms, which thus celebrated the divine "sonship" of Israel's davidic king:[36] the title spoke of the divine favor enjoyed by the king, as well as (no doubt) of the king's responsibility to carry out the divine mandate of establishing justice.[37]

Divine "sons" in intention, the davidic monarchs proved (on the whole) disappointingly human in the corruption with which they ruled. They were denounced by the prophets with the bitterness that betokens dashed ideals.[38] Prophets themselves foretold the fall of the Israelite kingdoms.[39] Still — we have seen this before — the dynamic of Israelite faith in a deity both powerful and benevolent did not allow that divine purposes could, in the end, be frustrated by human sin. Current davidic kings had proved unworthy of their calling; God would nonetheless fulfill his commitment to David and make of it — as intended — an instrument of his goodness. He would raise up in the future a righteous davidite to rule his people (or even the whole earth): evil would then be judged, foreign oppressors overthrown, fear banished, and peace would accompany justice.[40] The hope for such a "messiah" (or "anointed" king) was entertained by a number of pious Jews in the time of Jesus.[41] Since the davidites of old had been declared "God's son," it would be natural if the same title should be used of the coming davidic "messiah": and there is some evidence that this was done.[42]

34. 1 Samuel 8–31.

35. 2 Samuel 7:12-16.

36. See Psalm 2, esp. verse 7; Psalm 89:1-37, esp. verses 26-27; also Psalm 132.

37. See Psalm 72.

38. See, e.g., Jeremiah 22; Ezekiel 34.

39. The southern kingdom, Judah, retained a davidic monarch until its overthrow by the Babylonians.

40. See Isaiah 9:6-7; 11:1-10; Jeremiah 23:5-6; Ezekiel 34:23-31; Micah 5:2-4.

41. Note, however, that Israel's "messianic" hope included a *variety* of scenarios in which God would establish the rule of righteousness and restore the fortunes of his people; not all of them featured a davidic monarchy.

42. Note, in the New Testament, the apparent equivalence of the two titles in Mark 14:61; John 20:31.

Central to early *Christ*ian faith was the conviction that Jesus was God's *Christ* (the Greek equivalent of the Hebrew "messiah"), the one through whom God was intervening in history to end the sway of evil and establish the rule of righteousness and peace. That Messiah's atoning death was required for the transformation was at least not a common belief among Jews in Jesus' day. Sin and evil must certainly be dealt with; but a more standard script required only that God judge the wicked and deliver the righteous from their clutches. The early Christian drama implied, on the contrary, that *none* was fit to participate in God's rule apart from the atonement of his or her sin and a change of his or her heart's orientation: clearly a more radical view of human sin. At the same time, the divine intervention to establish peace and justice is also, in its Christian version, a signal demonstration of divine love, partly in the length to which it was prepared to go to redeem humanity (involving, as it did, the death of God's "anointed" and "son"), partly in its inclusiveness (*all* are seen as "ungodly," and atonement is made for the sins of *all*).

To conclude this summary of the Christian *messianic* drama, we need only note that in proclaiming Jesus as "Christ," the early Christians were by no means limiting his role to his sacrificial death for others. The risen Christ was declared to be "Lord,"[43] the one through whom God administers his righteous rule. Even now their exalted Lord was at God's "right hand."[44] The open manifestation of his reign, and the decisive judgment of all who continue to defy it, were believed to be reserved for a day when sinners had been given due opportunity to repent and the period of God's "forbearance" was finally over: then would come the rule of righteousness and peace for which all creation yearns.[45]

The designation "God's son" could thus be used as an equivalent of "God's messiah," the man appointed by God to bring about the triumph of the good. But Paul clearly means more by the title. Note, for example, how "Jesus Christ" is emphatically distinguished from human beings and classed (in some unspecified way) with God himself when Paul claims to be "an apostle with a commission neither originating with human beings, nor passed on by a human being, but given by

---

43. Acts 2:36; Romans 10:9; 1 Corinthians 12:3.

44. I.e., as God's effective administrator. See Acts 2:32-33; Ephesians 1:20-23.

45. Acts 3:19-21; 2 Peter 3:7-9.

Jesus Christ and God the Father."[46] Paul maintains the distinction throughout the verses that follow. He invokes divine blessing for human beings from "God our Father and the Lord Jesus Christ."[47] In carrying out his commission, Paul goes on to say, he could not please *people* and still serve *Christ*.[48] His gospel itself is not of human origin, nor was it communicated to him by any human being; it became his through a "revelation of Jesus Christ," a revelation of God's "son."[49] The whole argument will not allow that "God's son" is merely an honorary title for a human being with a divine mandate.[50]

Nor is it sufficient to say that for Paul the *man* Jesus had been exalted to something like divine status. While Paul certainly reckoned with the humanity of Jesus, he spoke of it as an adopted humanity, assumed for a divine purpose by one who himself existed previously "in the form of God."[51] Christ was "rich" before he became "poor" like us.[52] Romans is more explicit: "God accomplished what the law could not . . . by sending his son in flesh like our sinful flesh."[53] It is, indeed, crucial to Paul's argument and gospel that we see in the death of Jesus, not what a human being can do for God, but an expression of God's love for sinful humans.[54] The exaltation of the risen Jesus thus represents for Paul (as, of course, for the Fourth Gospel) a return to pre-incarnational glory.

---

46. Galatians 1:1.

47. Galatians 1:3. The double invocation is frequent in Paul.

48. Galatians 1:10.

49. Galatians 1:12, 16.

50. The passage (esp. Galatians 1:15-16) also suggests that it was the appearance to Paul of the resurrected Jesus in divine glory that compelled him to speak of Christ in more exalted terms; cf. 2 Corinthians 4:6, a verse that alludes to the same experience.

51. Philippians 2:5-7.

52. 2 Corinthians 8:9.

53. Romans 8:3. The quoted material literally ends "in the likeness of flesh of sin." The awkward phrase is meant to convey the point that Christ, though human, was, unlike other humans, without sin. Cf. 2 Corinthians 5:21 and (from a different early Christian author) Hebrews 4:15.

54. Romans 5:8. As we shall see in the next chapter, Paul does think that Christ's obedience *as a human being* overcame the effects of the sin of the first human being, Adam. But the very possibility of such "human" obedience depended on Christ's being something more than an offspring of Adam (see Romans 8:3). Hence the (human) obedience of Christ and its subsequent benefits are themselves spoken of as a gift of God's grace to humanity (Romans 5:15).

Paul's language of Christ's divine "sonship" therefore serves a number of purposes. It allows him to distinguish between Christ and the "Father" who sent him to reconcile sinners to himself. It suggests, moreover, the willing submission of the "son" to the "Father's" will.[55] At the same time, the term suggests that the divine "son" is distinct from ordinary human beings in sharing deity with the Father (as children share the "nature" of their parents).[56]

Obviously a fine line is being trod. Were we to say that only Paul's Jewish heritage kept him from speaking of two (or three!) gods, we would not do justice to the dynamic of his thinking: God, for the Christian Paul, continued to be *one,* the benevolent Creator of all. The life, death, and resurrection of Jesus Christ were significant precisely because they represented an intervention by God the Creator to redeem his sinful creatures: a second deity has no place in the scheme. Nor can Jesus be a mere man, however, if his self-sacrifice is to represent the decisive revelation of God the Creator's love and goodness toward humanity. Somehow terminology had to be found to express the conviction that creation and redemption are both the work of one God while allowing (what the Christian experience of God required) sufficient room for "otherness" within the deity to accommodate distinct roles within the same divine operations. Paul himself offers nothing more precise than the following formulations:

> For us there is one God, the Father, *from* whom are all things and *for* whom we ourselves exist, and one Lord, Jesus Christ, *through* whom are all things — indeed, we ourselves live *through* him.[57]

> God was active in Christ, reconciling the world to himself.[58]

> God proves his love for us in that, while we were still sinners, Christ died for us.[59]

---

55. Cf. 1 Corinthians 15:28; Galatians 1:4.

56. A more explicit ascription of deity to Christ may be found in Romans 9:5, a verse that — on its most natural reading — simply equates Christ with God; but other interpretations of the verse are possible. Cf. Colossians 2:9.

57. 1 Corinthians 8:6, italics mine.

58. 2 Corinthians 5:19.

59. Romans 5:8.

The later church, required to epitomize its faith, would refine this language and see in the eternal relationship between Father, Son, and Holy Spirit a delight in Otherness within the one deity that allows for the essence of God to be eternally that of love: before there were creatures for God to love, the Father loved the Son; the Son, the Father; both loved, and were loved by, the Holy Spirit. Such language carries us far beyond what we find in Paul, though, again, we may grant that it has roots in problems and features already found in the Pauline texts.

Romans 5:10 is not in any case concerned with christological doctrine. The point is rather that Christians can be sure of the bliss God has promised when they remember the length to which God was prepared to go to make it possible: they were "reconciled to God by the death of his son."[60]

---

60. Cf. the similar point in Romans 8:32.

Chapter 8

Freedom Versus Freedom

ROMANS 5:12–6:23

PERCEPTIVE READERS of the preceding chapters will harbor doubts whether Paul's notions of "freedom" can coincide with those of the modern West. Sympathetic readers will hasten to add that his failure to see things as we do is not, in itself, sufficient cause for dismissing his views as absurd. The task of this chapter will be to define "freedom" as Paul uses the term and to explore the logic that links it to his "Jewish-Christian"[1] horizons.

Notions of Freedom

Freedom, by any definition, implies an absence of constraint. Different horizons will determine what we regard as unwanted constraint.

If human beings are the only source of meaning, significant order, and value in the world,[2] then (it seems to many to follow that) they should be free to define for themselves what they find meaningful, to shape the order of their own existence, to pursue what they themselves choose to value. Apart from the social "contracts" that facilitate the coexistence of autonomous individuals, any externally imposed constraint on their freedom of choice seems unwarranted

---

1. For the sense in which I use the phrase, see Chapter One, n. 7.
2. See Chapter Two, n. 2 above.

69

and, for many,[3] unwanted. Authority, in a cosmos whose only order is mechanical, may well seem arbitrary, purely conventional, and infuriatingly restrictive: Why should the preferences of others set limits for *my* behavior? What lies in the way of autonomous individuals (provided it is not another autonomous individual) may legitimately be bulldozed for their convenience.

If, on the other hand, human beings are but a part of a larger whole whose meaning, purposeful order, and goodness is not their own creation, then bulldozing whatever obstructs their convenience[4] is a most ill-considered way to make their presence in the cosmos felt: partly because their own well-being depends on the integrity of the whole, partly because the goodness inherent in the whole and in each of its parts merits human esteem, and they show themselves stupid, insensitive, or mean when they disregard or destroy it. Humans thrive (on this perspective) as they embrace, celebrate, and pattern their lives according to the goodness of creation and the will of its Maker.

Authority, moreover, on this latter perspective, need hardly be arbitrary. Given the discrepancy between Pauline and contemporary ideals on this point, it is important to remind ourselves why.

If meaning, purposeful order, and goodness are inherent in the cosmos and humans have been blessed with the ability (in some measure) to grasp them, then the pursuit of truth is an inevitable and worthy human undertaking. People are not forfeiting their human freedom to an arbitrary ideal when they stubbornly search for the truth about any aspect of life in the cosmos. Quite the contrary. On the one hand, they are developing and expressing their powers as human beings with an innate drive for truth. On the other hand, they are giving truth the recognition it is due among creatures whose very contribution to the goodness of the cosmos is, in part, the capacity to perceive and affirm what is true.

Where truth is at issue, then, there is more to be said — in a purposefully and benevolently ordered cosmos — than that humans are

3. Dostoyevsky's "Grand Inquisitor" reminds us, however, that this is perhaps less true than we might be inclined to believe.

4. The metaphor is taken from Erazim Kohák's profound and beautiful book, *The Embers and the Stars: A Philosophical Inquiry into the Moral Sense of Nature* (Chicago: University of Chicago Press, 1984), p. 90. I hasten to add that my indebtedness to the book goes far beyond this particular adopted metaphor.

"free" to acknowledge *or* deny it, "free" to accept *or* defy its implications. More is at stake than "freedom of choice" when people choose to lie, cheat, or slander; to take for themselves what others' work has made their own; to engage in the deeply personal intimacies of the procreative act, thus implying a commitment both to one's partner in intimacy and to the potential offspring of the union, without giving substance to such a commitment.[5] Those who would live in harmony with reality cannot sin, in these ways and others, against the truth.[6] Conversely, those who choose to lie — in word or deed — are betraying the very goodness of the cosmos and of their place within it.

Furthermore, if the order of the cosmos is one of goodness, then goodness, too, has its own inherent authority. There are, Paul insists, no "self-made" people: "What do you have that you did not receive? And if you received it, why do you brag as though you did not receive it?"[7] If people do not live by their own resources, they can claim no "right" to live selfishly for their own interests.[8] Goodness obligates its beneficiaries. But the authority of goodness to compel human recognition and response is not a mere matter of reciprocating favors. Humans have been blessed with the capacity to appreciate beauty, to recognize and pursue ideals of kindness, courage, loyalty, and love.[9] People are not forfeiting their human freedom to arbitrary ideals when they acknowledge and practice virtue. Rather, they are developing and expressing their powers as human beings with a yearning for what is good, and giving what is good the esteem it is due. There is, then, once again, more to be said — in a purposefully and benevolently ordered universe — than that humans are free to acknowledge or defy these ideals. More is at stake than "freedom of choice" when people live in disregard of their neighbor's need, or when they exploit, oppress, or do violence to others of God's creatures. Such deeds sin against the truth that all are a part of God's creation and against the goodness of creation of which all have received and which humans were made with the faculty — and the duty — to embrace.

Love, too, has authority — if the universe is steered by divine love.

5. See the discussion of marriage in Chapter Four above.
6. See 2 Corinthians 13:8.
7. 1 Corinthians 4:7.
8. See Romans 14:7.
9. See Philippians 4:8.

For Paul, God's love for people *compels* them in turn to live for God and others; they are called upon not to look out for their own interests, but for the interests of others.[10] Again, more is at stake than "freedom of choice" when people refuse, on the one hand, to trust and submit to divine love, and, on the other, to reflect that love to others. They are betraying — and turning their backs on the chance to know — the love that undergirds their existence while they attempt to de- and reconstruct God's world to their own specifications. Those who sin against divine love reject a home in the cosmos it steers.

Different horizons, different freedoms. Insistence on freedom of personal choice in defiance of any universal norms seems — to many, at least — appropriate in what they take to be a purely material, mechanically run universe. But freedom can be enjoyed in a cosmos that is purposefully and benevolently ordered as well: the options and opportunities open to those who would pursue truth, goodness, and love are diverse and innumerable. What cripples and incapacitates humans from finding fulfillment in such a cosmos is precisely the insistence on personal autonomy, the prioritizing of personal choice above the claims of truth, goodness, and love. From their disastrous enslavement to the lie of their own independence, the self-absorbed need to be set *free*.

Adam and the Constraint of Sin

In the well-known story of Genesis 3, the lie that — according to the "Jewish-Christian" worldview — bedevils the human condition originates with Adam and Eve. They live in, and are themselves a part of, a created order that is declared "very good."[11] Within that order they enjoy a privileged position, made in the "image" of God and exercising on his behalf authority over other creatures.[12] They are placed in a garden

---

10. 2 Corinthians 5:14-15; Philippians 2:4. Paul's words are, of course, directed to Christians, and the demand that they live for others has a particular force for those who believe that God's son has died for them. But he no doubt sees such a life as God's design for all humanity.

11. Genesis 1:31.

12. Genesis 1:26.

pleasant to behold and bountiful in its provisions.[13] Their options are multitudinous — and all but one of them are good. Only a single command has been given them so that they can acknowledge by their obedience their status as creatures in God's world: they are not to eat of the "tree of the knowledge of good and evil."[14] They eat, of course, distrusting the goodness of God and desiring to be "gods" themselves.[15] And so "sin entered the world."[16]

That the story of Adam[17] is in some sense the story of us all is certainly part of Paul's point in Romans 5:12-21, but the relationship between the wrongdoing of our progenitor and that of his discredited brood is not altogether clear. Romans 5:12 by itself might suggest simply that Adam was the first sinner, that his act introduced sin and death into our world, and that the rest of us share his fate inasmuch as we sin as he did. Adam, on such a reading, did us the disservice of setting a very bad precedent — but we are fools to follow. We are under no particular pressure to do so. Each of us, in our own several ways, reenacts the disobedience and fall of our forebear in the Garden of Eden.

But such cannot be Paul's meaning. If we *all* do things we ought not to do,[18] then there is, it would seem, more to be said of the human condition than that individuals make bad choices. The same conclusion follows if God is nowhere given the acknowledgment he is due. Paul speaks in Romans 5:19 of the disobedience of Adam as the means by which others "were made sinners."[19] The implication is clearly that, when people commit sins, they are not falling from innocence in the same way that Adam did, but rather giving expression to a sinfulness characteristic of their Adamic humanity. People can even be said to "live

13. Genesis 2:8-9, 15.

14. Genesis 2:17.

15. Genesis 3:4-6.

16. Romans 5:12.

17. Paul ignores the role of Eve in his references to the Genesis story in Romans 5:12-21, no doubt because he wants to focus on the comparison between Adam and Christ. Cf. 1 Corinthians 15:21-22, 45; and contrast the reference to Eve in 2 Corinthians 11:3 (where the Adam-Christ typology is not in view).

18. Romans 5:12.

19. The "many" of whom Paul speaks are, of course, all Adam's "descendants," or all humankind.

in sin":[20] sin is the sphere within which they act and think; it fixes the boundaries of their horizons. They choose to do and are responsible for the particular sins that they commit. That they commit sins is, however, an inevitable consequence of their living a life defined (in part at least) by "sin."

Yet, however rooted in human nature sin may be, it cannot be "natural" and still be "sin." "Sin" is, necessarily, a distortion of what ought to be; and, necessarily, the distortion involved in "sin" is that of resistance to God, to his will, and to the goodness of his creation. Paul believes that people remain aware, at some level, of the wrongfulness of much of what they do, and desire, at some level, to do better. In this sense there is within every human being an "I" that recognizes a goodness not of its own creation or definition and longs to embrace it. Yet such is the hold of sin upon people's lives that they cannot yield the truly good more than fitful acknowledgment. They are sin's slaves — paradoxically, both with and without their will. So Paul depicts the disordered personality of Adamic humanity.[21]

How are we to understand Paul's notion of "sin" that is prior to particular sins? That is rooted and universal in human nature while remaining a distortion of what ought to be? That enslaves its subjects? Whenever one deliberately chooses *not* to do what (at some level) one acknowledges ought to be done, and whenever one deliberately chooses to *do* what (at some level) one acknowledges ought not to be done, more is involved than succumbing to the lure of a particular temptation. One is expressing the priority one gives to one's own choosing over one's respect for the goodness of the created order. In effect, one is staking out one's claim to be "god," to reshape creation to one's liking, to determine "good and evil" for oneself. This human appropriation of

---

20. Romans 6:1-2.

21. I have drawn in this paragraph on Romans 7:15-24. Some interpreters, however, think that this passage has in view the continued moral struggles of the Christian. They think it unlikely that Paul would attribute to Adamic humanity a desire for what is good. I (together with many other interpreters) find more improbable that he could depict Christian existence as one of being "sold under sin" (Romans 7:14; contrast Romans 6:18, 22), powerless to deal with the "flesh" (Romans 7:18; contrast Romans 8:9), engaged in a struggle with sin in which God's spirit plays no evident part (note the absence of any reference to God's spirit in 7:15-24; and contrast Romans 8:3-4, 9). See further Chapter Nine below.

divine prerogatives means, of necessity, that God himself is not being given his due, that one is acting apart from faith in him. These are *moral* choices, choices that (according to the "Jewish-Christian" worldview) are wrongly made. And certainly one can imagine created, intelligent beings (such as the angels who serve God in the biblical tradition) who choose differently. Yet such choices *are* made, and have been made throughout human history. Humanity is marked by its insistence on choosing its own course of action and by the expression of this insistence in deeds it knows to be wrong.

At some point some human being or beings with sufficient grasp of the options before them must have been the first to make a morally *wrong* choice. But the human condition (Paul believes) is not now what it was then. The orientation adopted by those who first committed sin seems now a fixture in human nature. The self-absorption, the insistence on self-rule, the lack of faith in God that take expression in particular sins are all part and parcel of the human condition — though (and this is essential) they are just as wrong, and just as much a distortion of the way humans were meant to live, as ever. However common deceit, jealousy, strife, and violence may be, they remain sin, and the world in which they occur is not the world as it ought to be. Humans still owe God the wholehearted trust and obedience due his goodness — though, slaves of sin that they are, they are both unable and unwilling to give it.[22] Sin "lives" in them.[23] It dogs them even when they feel a desire to do the good.[24] If it seems dormant for a time, it leaps to resistance when it encounters a divine commandment.[25] Apart from a divine transformation, humanity's bent for sin is incorrigible.

Can Adamic humanity do *anything* good? Yes, Paul would say — and No. Paul recognizes (as we have seen) that people have moral sensibilities that in some measure continue to reflect the truth about their position in the world; and he does not deny that they sometimes act in accordance with these sensibilities.[26] On the other hand, he believes that sin has taken radical root in human nature. The blunt truth

22. Romans 8:7-8.
23. Romans 7:17.
24. Romans 7:21.
25. Romans 7:8-9.
26. For Paul's recognition of pagan moral sensibilities, see, in addition to Romans 2, Romans 12:17; 14:18; 1 Corinthians 5:1; 2 Corinthians 8:21.

of the matter, as Paul sees it, seems to be this: people do much that would be both good and God-pleasing were it done as an expression of their wholehearted faith in him. Yet even such deeds cannot, finally, be either God-pleasing or good when they represent the mere coincidental overlap between the divinely ordered good and the behavior adopted by a self that, at its deepest roots, is determined to pursue its own goals. "Whatever is not an expression of faith is sin."[27]

The Rule of Death

With sin comes death: for Paul,[28] Genesis,[29] and biblical tradition as a whole, the two belong together. Greed, anger, malice, lust, and the like are seen as sins against life as it was meant to be. They intrude upon and disfigure the innocence of creation and wreak havoc and death within it.[30] God will not sustain forever the life of those who choose to live independently of him and in defiance of love; nor will he give them long to mar his handiwork. The soul that sins, dies. Indeed, the whole created order sullied by sin has been subjected to decay and death.[31] Were it to continue forever in its disfigured state, the Creator's designs for its goodness would be foiled.

Nor, in biblical terminology, is the "death" linked to sin merely physical. Indeed, in the Hebrew Scriptures, physical death is not always regarded as an evil: not, for example, when a patriarch dies "in a good old age . . . full of years,"[32] particularly if he has been able to bounce great-grandchildren upon his knees.[33] Still, death brings an end to the activities

---

27. Romans 14:23. The principle seems true to Paul, even though its original application in Romans 14 is more limited. A similar perspective is apparent in the well-known dominical words of Matthew 7:17-18: "Thus every good tree yields good fruit, whereas every rotten tree yields bad fruit. A good tree cannot yield bad fruit, nor can a rotten tree yield good."

28. Romans 5:12.

29. Genesis 2:17.

30. See, most graphically, Genesis 6:11-13.

31. Romans 8:20.

32. Genesis 25:8.

33. Genesis 50:23.

and relationships one has known, even — as the psalmists are wont to point out — to the joy of praising God.[34] Moreover, death is said to cast its shadow over the still living when disease or distress prevents them from knowing the cheers of normal human existence.[35] In such cases we may speak of a kind of "spiritual" death. To be delivered from such distress is spoken of as an escape from death, and the psalmists who know the experience are exuberant in their praise of the divine Life-Giver.[36]

The psalmists' relish for life is clearly rooted in their sense of being "at home" in an ordered, benevolent cosmos. They acknowledge that it is God who has "made us, and not we ourselves,"[37] that "we are his people, and the sheep of his pasture," that he is "good" and worthy of trust and praise.[38] To refuse God recognition is to quit the cosmic dance, to make do on one's own in a world whose goodness is a gift of love to be celebrated with all God's creatures.[39] The psalmists see nothing admirable or splendid in those who choose the path of isolation: only self-absorption,[40] mulish stubbornness,[41] incredible folly,[42] a slippery pathway,[43] and certain doom.[44] Nor is death only a fate that awaits them; already they have cut themselves off from life as it was meant to be lived.[45]

In short, when Paul wrote, "The wages of sin is death,"[46] he was merely giving epigrammatic expression to a principle basic to the "Jewish-Christian" worldview.

To sum up the principles of Paul's perspective:

1. Humans were made to enjoy a privileged position in a world created good.

---

34. See Psalm 6:5; 88:10-12; 115:17; Isaiah 38:18. I noted in Chapter Four that belief in an afterlife is not found in much of the Hebrew Bible.

35. Psalm 18:4-5; 31:9-13; 88:3-18.

36. Psalm 116:1-19; see also Psalm 9:13-14; 56:10-13; Isaiah 38:15-20.

37. Or "made us, and his we are."

38. Psalm 100 (King James Version).

39. See, e.g., Psalm 148.

40. Psalm 10:4; 12:3-4.

41. Psalm 32:9.

42. Psalm 14:1; 94:6-11.

43. Psalm 73:18.

44. Psalm 37:12-13, 20, 35-36, 38.

45. See Psalm 32:3-4.

46. Romans 6:23.

2. Humans have fallen from the "glory" for which they were intended[47] through their refusal to acknowledge and trust God, their determination to pursue their own (self-defined) good.

3. Such was the choice of Adam. His sin marked out the boundaries within which humanity lives. People choose, commit, and are responsible for their own individual sins. In so doing, however, they are merely giving personal expression to the will to self-rule that characterizes the whole human race.

4. Humans retain enough of a sense of the good to know that they have sinned against it, and indeed desire, at some level, to do what is right. Their sin thus remains a sin against the truth, a living lie that destroys the sinner's integrity.

5. Sin kills.

A New Human Prototype

Jesus Christ was (1) a man of a different ilk, (2) introduced by God (3) into Adamic humanity (4) to offset the sin of Adam and (5) to liberate Adam's offspring from the tyranny of sin and death. Those who belong to Christ (6) enjoy freedom from sin's rule, though it is a freedom that (7) must be practiced to be maintained.

1. As we saw in the last chapter, Jesus was, for Paul, more than a man: he was God's "son" sent "in human flesh like our sinful flesh" to condemn and overcome sin.[48] That he was God's son accounts for his capacity (not otherwise found in Adamic humanity) to overcome sin and live a life characterized by radical trust and obedience toward God.[49] But such — it must be remembered — was the life for which *all* humanity was intended; it needed, therefore, to be lived by one who was human if the divine purposes for humanity were to be realized. God's "son" though he was, Christ was also, and needed to be, a *man* to counter the sin of the man Adam and restore his descendants to the life humans were made to enjoy.

47. Romans 3:23.
48. Romans 8:3.
49. See Romans 5:19.

For since death came through a man, through a man came also the resurrection of the dead. For as in Adam all die, so in Christ all will be made alive.[50]

2. The life and death of Christ as a man, and the possibility he procured for humanity to be delivered from sin and restored to God's favor, are all gifts of God's grace. Paul does not begrudge the ink required to underline the point.[51]

3. Humanity apart from Christ is "in Adam," living in conditions determined by Adam's sin: slaves themselves of sin, cut off from God's favor, subject to condemnation and death. Jesus lived in a body and under conditions like those under which other humans sin.

4. Christ, however, obeyed God throughout (and, in the end, at the cost of) his life. He thus, "in the flesh," overcame and condemned the "sin in the flesh" to which other human beings succumb:[52] such sin is, in his case, a defeated power. Having died, he left the sphere over which sin exercises its tyranny. Having risen again, he lives for God no longer encumbered by the weaknesses and temptations to which humanity on a sin-scarred earth is inevitably subject.[53] It behooves humanity to somehow be detached from the conditions of life that resulted from Adam's disobedience and to share the possibilities of a different life opened up by Christ's obedience.

5. God refuses to abandon his creatures to the power of evil. His purpose is to rescue humanity through Christ. To accomplish this end, he has ordained that Adamic human beings can, by baptism, be "united with Christ." Their baptism marks them out as those who, with Jesus, have died to sin[54] and now share new life in God's service.[55] The baptized are no longer "Adam-people" but, by a divine transference, "Christ-

---

50. 1 Corinthians 15:21-22.
51. Romans 5:15-21.
52. Romans 8:3.
53. Romans 6:10.
54. For the notion, see, in addition to Romans 6, Galatians 2:19-20; 5:24; 6:14; also 2 Corinthians 4:10. The implication, of course, is that Adamic humanity cannot be fitted for God's kingdom by adjustments here and improvements there. To prescribe repentance and new resolutions is no remedy. The self corrupted by sin must die and new life be given (by God, of course: see Romans 4:17) in its place.
55. Romans 6:3-11.

people," members of the new humanity[56] whose terms of existence are defined not by Adam's disobedience, but by the obedience and righteousness of Christ.

6. Those who have "died to sin" have been set free from its tyranny.[57] While they clung to their self-rule and self-absorption, they could not lose themselves in God's love, embrace and delight in his goodness, or know the sense of "belonging" in a cosmos steered by his benevolence. From such a life of goodness, Paul says (with deliberate irony) that they were "free."[58] To the constraints of their life in sin, by the intervention of God's grace, they have now "died"; now they find themselves enjoying a new freedom, empowered by the spirit of Christ, with countless possibilities of service and celebration to be explored throughout an endless life.[59]

7. But the *earthly* life of believers has an interim character. They have "died" — with Christ — to sin, they have been set free from the lie of their independence and the insistence on self-rule. They are assured of life — with Christ — and have already experienced the presence of the "Holy Spirit" as a power for good and a foretaste of divine favors still to come. Nonetheless, they continue to live in a body exposed to the temptations of sin. And though they are not likely to renounce the new life for the old, there is a risk that they will try to combine the two. Can one not (they may suppose) "continue in sin," not out of defiance toward God, but — on the contrary — trusting in his unlimited grace?[60]

Such a marriage of heaven and hell is not an option. Sin enslaves and leads to death. Goodness and life in God's service are open only to those who have renounced self-rule, who have "died" to sin: for them continued acquiescence in its thraldom is inconceivable.[61] That believers struggle with temptation is presupposed throughout Romans 6. That they can succumb to its lure, be "overtaken" by particular sins, and need restoration was an experience with which Paul was clearly familiar.[62]

56. See also 2 Corinthians 5:17.
57. Romans 6:7, 18, 22.
58. Romans 6:20.
59. Romans 7:6; 8:9.
60. Romans 6:1.
61. Romans 6:2.
62. Galatians 6:1.

That becoming like Christ is a transformation taking place (not without stops and starts, falls and new beginnings) over a lifetime[63] and more[64] is self-evident. But would-be believers cannot reembrace the lie of their own independence or effectively insist on self-rule by giving themselves to the pursuit of sin without losing the freedom they now purportedly enjoy.[65]

63. 2 Corinthians 3:18.
64. Philippians 3:20-21.
65. Romans 6:16.

Chapter 9

The Goals and Goodness of the Law

ROMANS 7:1–8:13

PABLO CASALS used to decry the "bad German tradition" that treated Bach as "Herr Professor" and regarded his unaccompanied cello suites as nothing more than musical exercises. Casals himself brought a passion to their performance that opened the eyes of many to their awesome power: the power of the "terrifying Bach,"[1] of Bach the "volcano" — whom "purists" would reduce to a "professor"![2]

Paul needs a Pablo Casals. He was no more a professor than was Bach — nor are his letters less dynamic than the latter's suites. A dispassionate reconstruction of Paul's views of sin, of Christ's love, of "redemption" and "salvation" can hardly breed an understanding of Paul or make his impact comprehensible. "Paul and the law" has become a topic for academic debate. For Paul it was anything but academic. We begin by asking why.

1. So Casals quoted Mendelson — with approval!
2. References are taken from "Casals: A Living Portrait," a Columbia Masterworks recording (no date given).

God of Moses — God of Christ Jesus

For Paul, the law was "holy," its "commandment holy, righteous, and good."[3] The terms permit definition, but Paul's point can scarcely be grasped from within the "disenchanted" horizons of the modern West. If, for us, the world is purely material, its order no more than mechanical, then — to understand Paul — we will need to recapture the vision of a cosmos fashioned and steered by divine goodness, and of human beings as an integral part of its order. That the law is "holy" then means that it originates with the divinely Other. That what it demands is "righteous and good" means that it rightly reflects the situation of humanity in the cosmos and, if obeyed, will prove conducive to life and well-being. That God gave such a gift to Israel must, from such a perspective, be reckoned among the greatest proofs of his love.[4] Sympathetic readers of Psalm 119 will grasp something of the treasured place occupied by Torah[5] for those whose horizons included the holy and the good and who saw Torah's laws as their embodiment.

Paul was certainly among them. Prior to his adoption of the Christian cause, he excelled his contemporaries in his devotion to the law.[6] Nor did his coming to Christian "faith" do anything to alter his convictions about the sacredness of Torah's demands. On the contrary: it was essential to Paul's understanding of Christ that his death expressed the love for sinners of the same God who created them and whose benevolent will they had defied. The God of Christ Jesus was also the God of Moses: but Moses could no longer be seen as the locus of his decisive revelation.

In Deuteronomy (as we have seen), Israel's enjoyment of life and divine blessing depended on their obedience to the will of God revealed in the Torah.[7] For Paul (as we have also seen), enjoyment of life and

3. Romans 7:12.

4. Romans 3:1-2; 9:4; cf. Psalm 147:19-20.

5. The term here refers to the sum of commands and prohibitions, with the accompanying sanctions, believed to have been given by God to Israel (through the agency of Moses) on Mount Sinai. See Chapter Four above.

6. Such, to be sure, is his own claim (Galatians 1:14); but the passion and single-mindedness he brought to his Christian apostleship leave no reason to doubt his self-perception on this point.

7. See Chapter Four above.

divine blessing is dependent on faith in Christ.[8] The latter conviction — forced upon Paul, he believed, by a personal revelation of God's son — necessarily required a reevaluation of the place of Torah in the divine agenda. In what follows I will attempt a summary of its results.

The Righteousness of the Law

Paul remained convinced that Torah had been divinely given; indeed, a display of divine glory accompanied its promulgation.[9] From such a conviction follow both the character of Torah's commands as "holy, righteous, and good" and the inevitability of a divine purpose in imposing them.

Torah's commands were all "righteous" and "good," but their "righteousness" and "goodness" were of different kinds.[10] Paul does not draw explicit distinctions in his writings. Nonetheless, when he speaks of Gentile observance of the law, of its "work" as "written" on Gentile "hearts" and attested by their "conscience,"[11] he is clearly referring to the *moral* demands of the Mosaic law: Gentiles, too, know that it is wrong to murder, commit adultery, steal. Clearly Paul did not think that Gentiles were aware of, or subject to, an obligation to keep Israel's food or festival laws. The same exclusive focus on the law's moral demands may well be present in Paul's insistence that Christians are enabled by the divine spirit to fulfill "the righteous demand of the law,"[12] and that "love is the fulfillment of the law."[13] The "righteousness" and "goodness" of these demands of the law lie in their effective formulation of behavior appropriate to all human beings living in God's world, behavior that conforms to the universal requirements of truth, goodness, and love.

8. See Chapter Six above.

9. 2 Corinthians 3:7.

10. See, again, the discussion on "The Place of Law in Deuteronomy" in Chapter Four above.

11. Romans 2:14-15, 26-27.

12. Romans 8:4. Alternatively, the "righteous demand" (singular) of the law may be for that faith and obedience toward God implicit in all of the law's particular demands.

13. Romans 13:8-10; cf. Galatians 5:14. Note, in Romans 13:9, that it is moral demands that are cited as "summed up" in the love command.

But the law also contains commands of circumcision, of festival observance, and of permitted and forbidden foods that Paul insisted were *not* to be imposed upon Gentiles even when they became members (together with Jewish Christians) in the "people of God." The "righteousness" and "goodness" of such demands[14] lay in the opportunity their imposition presented to Jews to express obedience and trust in God in all areas of their lives. These commands, however, were given only to Jews. In Paul's view (shared by many Jews), it was inherent neither in their nature nor in the divine purpose that they should be universalized.

The Weakness of the Law

The Israel to whom the law was given belonged to Adamic humanity. Favored though it was, Israel continued to be marked by the Adamic refusal to trust God and submit to his will. In Pauline terminology, the law encountered, and could not overcome, the "flesh."

Paul can speak of life "in the flesh" in a neutral way, meaning the embodied existence of human beings.[15] Given, however, that what has come to determine the character of such "life in the flesh" is humanity's resistance to God, Paul can also use the word "flesh" to refer to humanity's incorrigible bent for sin:[16] nothing good lives in the "flesh";[17] the "flesh" is at war with God's spirit;[18] it does not, and cannot, submit to God's law;[19] those who are "in the flesh" cannot please God.[20]

Paul dramatizes the encounter between God's "law" and the "flesh"

---

14. Paul himself does not address this issue. The view here summarized was standard among Jews. Allegorical interpretations of the significance of such laws were also common among Jews of Paul's day (e.g., forbidden foods might be seen as symbols for various vices). The latter interpretations, of course, ran the risk of undercutting the importance of literal observance of the law.

15. Romans 9:3, 5; Galatians 2:20.

16. Note Paul's play on the two senses of "flesh" in 2 Corinthians 10:3.

17. Romans 7:18.

18. Galatians 5:17.

19. Romans 8:7.

20. Romans 8:8.

in Romans 7:7-13, then explains its outcome in 7:14-25. Though he speaks in the first person of what "I" have experienced, the account is intended to be generic, not strictly autobiographical; a clarification of the role played by the law in humanity's enslavement to sin that nonetheless maintains the goodness of its commands.[21] The "I" is, throughout the section, a creature of "flesh" whose horizons are defined by the sinful orientation of Adamic humanity. For a time, perhaps, the sin that insists on self-rule and refuses to trust and submit to God may lie dormant ("dead," in the terminology of Romans 7:8): for just so long, that is, as the "I" does not find itself confronted with a divine command. When such a confrontation takes place, however, a disastrous outcome is inevitable. Not that the law is responsible — God forbid! There is nothing wrong (Paul insists) with the law or its commands. If rightly embraced in a spirit of trust and obedience, they would lead to life.[22] Such, however, is not the mind-set of Adamic humanity. Its innate rebelliousness and insistence on self-rule spring to life when demands for obedience are placed upon it.[23] Whatever lingering awareness there may be of a good that is not self-defined, whatever yearning there may be to pursue it, it is sin, in the end, that rules the day.[24] The commandment, the observance of which would bring life, is transgressed. The result is death.[25]

Such an understanding of "what happens" when God's law "meets" the sinful "flesh" underlies other claims about what *has* happened to Israel after it was entrusted with the law. Paul concludes his portrayal of humanity's sin[26] with the claim that those to whom the law was given have "gone astray" from God no less than have the Gentiles. The giving of the law has thus resulted, not in a vital relationship between Israel

---

21. Note the questions that Paul is attempting to answer in Romans 7:7, 13. His statement in Romans 7:9-10 in particular is hard to explain as a strictly autobiographical statement. The discrepancy between the utter despair of ever doing the good exhibited by the "I" of Romans 7:15-25 and Paul's own "robust conscience" as exhibited in Philippians 3:4-6 is also frequently cited as evidence that the former description is not primarily autobiographical.

22. Romans 7:10.

23. Romans 7:7-11.

24. Romans 7:15-25.

25. Romans 7:10.

26. Romans 1:18–3:20.

and God marked by Israel's wholehearted trust and obedience, but in an indictment of universal human sinfulness.[27] Elsewhere he speaks of the law and the covenant of which it is a part as bringing divine wrath,[28] a divine curse,[29] condemnation and death.[30] The assumption throughout is that even the most favored segment of Adamic humanity rebels against God; by transgressing God's law, Israel has activated the negative sanctions that accompany its commands.[31]

What led Paul to so pessimistic a judgment? Three factors are key.

First and ultimately decisive must have been the Christian belief that salvation was to be found in Christ, who had died for the sins of humanity. From such a conviction, which Paul adopted as divine revelation, it followed that the path to life of a conformity with the law had been divinely declared nonviable, and, further, that sin constituted the dilemma from which Christ provided deliverance.

Second, Paul inherited a long tradition that saw Israel's waywardness as incorrigible. Inherent in such a tradition was the belief not only that Israel's sins required atonement, but that Israel's sinful bent required transformation before God's people could ever satisfactorily fulfill God's law.

To revelation and tradition we should certainly add observation as a third factor in Paul's judgment. Romans 7:7-25 is not primarily autobiographical; but it seems most unlikely that Paul had no personal experience of the dilemma he there describes in the first person. No doubt his Christian convictions have colored his depiction of the inability of the sinful "I" to do the good. But he can hardly have been exempt from the widely attested sense of frustration that accompanies serious moral endeavor — particularly when he has himself provided as graphic an account of it as any. Even with the best of intentions (Paul must have judged from his own experience), human beings fall short of the goodness that they know they ought to show.[32]

27. Romans 3:19-20.
28. Romans 4:15.
29. Galatians 3:10, 13.
30. 2 Corinthians 3:7, 9.
31. See also Romans 5:13, 20; 7:5; 8:2; 1 Corinthians 15:56.
32. Philippians 3:6 does not rule out such a reading of Paul. The text is not in any case a claim to sinless perfection, but only to a serious attempt to observe the law, including its prescribed rites of atonement for shortcomings. This attempt would have

Thus, when Paul needs to explain why the gift of the divine law has not brought life as it promises, he says simply that those subject to the law have not met its conditions, its demands for obedience. Romans 3:27-31 suggests, however, two additional reasons why observance of the law could not have been the divinely intended means for people to secure good relations with God.

The second reason is not controversial — at least with regard to our understanding of Paul's point. The law was given to Jews. But God is not the God of Jews only. One would expect the God of all the earth to open a path to fellowship with himself that puts all peoples on an equal footing. Such is the path, not of the law, but of faith.[33]

The first reason is that the law, with its demand for deeds in compliance with its terms, allows for human boasting,[34] and Paul believes that human boasting before God is inappropriate.[35] Controversy surrounds the type of boasting Paul has in mind. Is it boasting on the part of those entrusted with the law in their special status as implied by the gift? Or is it boasting of human achievement on the part of those who believe that they have observed the law and so secured a place in God's favor? In support of the former position is the reference to Jewish boasting in Romans 2:17, where the focus, as the context shows, is on divine privileges granted to Israel. But the second position seems stronger. Paul notes in Romans 3:27 that while boasting is invited by a law demanding "works," it is excluded if the pathway to divine favor is that of faith.[36] He is clearly pursuing the same point at the beginning of chapter 4. Abraham would

---

been deemed to have passed muster (hence "blameless") among adherents of the "righteousness of the law." Note too, however, that Paul is here bent on undercutting the pretensions to faithful observance of the law of people whose zeal in no way (he believed) approximated his own. The argument calls for evidence of Paul's erstwhile devotion to the law; it need not exclude an experience of moral struggle such as that attested in Romans 7.

33. Romans 3:29-30.

34. Romans 3:27-28.

35. Cf. 1 Corinthians 1:26-31; Galatians 6:14.

36. The "law of faith" in this verse means the "principle of faith": Paul is playing with different senses of the word *law*. Some interpreters do take the "law of faith" to be a reference to the Mosaic law, noting that the demand that underlies all of its particular demands is for faith in God. It seems unlikely, however, that Paul is making such a point in this passage, since here he repeatedly *contrasts* the "law" (or the "works of the law") with "faith" (Romans 3:21-22, 28, 31; 4:13-14).

have been entitled to boast if he had enjoyed divine approval on the basis of his "works": such approval, after all, would have represented, not a gift of divine grace, but compensation for work that he had done. In reality, however, Abraham's approval was an act of the grace of God who approves the ungodly when they trust in him. This expansion of the claim introduced in Romans 3:27 shows that Paul regards the path of faith, of utter dependence upon God, as one that rules out boasting in human achievement; on the other hand, any path involving human "works" (and that necessarily includes that of the law, with its demand for "works") invites boasting. Paul's sense of the appropriate stance of humans before God then requires that faith, not "works," be the principle by which humans enjoy good relations with their Maker.[37]

Why, Then, the Law?

Adamic human beings, characterized by the priority that they assign self-rule over the demands of truth, goodness, and love, were not likely to change their orientation when confronted by a law telling them what they ought to do. Why, then, we may ask, did God bother giving such a law?

Perhaps we need, first, to note again Paul's continued insistence that the law *was* a gift of God's goodness and a peculiar favor entrusted to Israel.[38] That Jews did not obey the law in no way alters its character as "holy," or that of its commands as "holy, righteous, and good."[39] There is a holiness, a rightness, and a goodness in stating the truth about humans and their place in God's world that is not affected by their response.[40]

---

37. Cf. Ephesians 2:8-9. (Note, however, that scholars debate whether Ephesians was written by Paul or by someone close to him writing in his name.) The reluctance to see Paul as concerned about boasting in one's observance of the law appears to me to be largely rooted in a commendable desire to undercut a stereotypical depiction of Jews as self-righteous and boastful. It should be emphasized that Paul does not appear to regard Jews as distinguished by a propensity to boasting peculiar to themselves. *Any* boasting of the "flesh" (i.e., of Adamic humanity) before God he finds inappropriate.

38. Romans 3:1-2; 9:3-4.

39. Romans 3:3; 7:12.

40. For the sentiment, see Ezekiel 2:3-5.

But it is also (Paul would say) good that sin be identified as such and condemned. Sin was present in the world and worked its deadly bane throughout the period from Adam to Moses, even before the law was given:[41] murder, adultery, and theft did not first become wrong when the decalogue proscribed them. But the giving of the law served to mark out such sin as transgression: as the willful violation of concrete, specified, legitimate demands.[42] Deeds that were wrong in any case now represented the deliberate flaunting of God's commands.[43] Indeed (as noted earlier in this chapter), when the rebellious "flesh" encountered God's law, its inchoate rebelliousness acquired a focus against which it could define its defiance, and sin multiplied.[44] But though the spread of sin cannot be considered in positive terms, the definition, recognition,[45] and indictment[46] of its mutinous character are good, even necessary steps in the ultimate banishment of all that corrupts the goodness of God's creation.[47]

The Fulfillment of the Law

Paul adamantly insists that the law's demand of circumcision is not to be imposed upon Gentile Christians.[48] He declares that the period of

41. Romans 5:13-14.

42. Romans 4:15.

43. To illustrate the point: in Jason's household it is considered wrong for him to help himself to cookies without asking. The defiance involved in such an act is multiplied, however, if he has just been told that the freshly baked cookies on the table have been made for a party and must not be touched. In particular periods of rebelliousness, such a recognized opportunity to defy a parent's edict may in fact be more determinative of his conduct than the lure of the chocolate chips in the cookies.

44. Romans 5:20; 7:5, 7-13.

45. See Romans 3:20; 7:7.

46. Romans 4:15.

47. Paul would also have shared the early Christian conviction that Israel's sacrificial cult as ordained in Torah served the positive function of "foreshadowing" (i.e., of providing an interpretive framework for the significance of) Christ's death. See the discussion of "Early Christian Perspectives" in Chapter Five above. When he asks why the law was given, however, he has in mind its moral demands (see Romans 3:20; 5:20; Galatians 3:19).

48. The letter to the Galatians was written to make this point. It is also reflected in Romans 4:9-17.

the law's validity ended with the coming of Christ,[49] and claims in various ways that believers are no longer subject to its commands and sanctions: they have "died to the law,"[50] have been "set free" from the law,[51] are no longer "under" the law,[52] and have been "redeemed" from its sway.[53] All of this would be perfectly straightforward were it not also clear that Paul expected Christian behavior to comply with the moral demands of the law.[54] Indeed, his letters are remarkably well stocked with prescriptions for believers' behavior, many of them overlapping with the demands of the Mosaic law. Not surprisingly, a number of scholars have announced a breakdown in apostolic logic at this point.

Others have rushed to the apostle's defense with a distinction that would preserve his consistency: Paul believed, they suggest, that Christians were no longer bound by the *ritual* or *ceremonial* demands of the law (for example, those involving circumcision, food, and festival observances), though they were still subject to its *moral* commands. The suggestion is both simple and plausible, and may claim as support those passages in which Paul speaks simply of "the law" while intending only its moral component.[55] Perhaps it is the best we can make of a complex point in the Pauline corpus. To my mind, however, neither the charge of inconsistency nor the defense that limits Christian freedom from the law to an exemption from its ritual demands[56] does justice to an important Pauline theme.

Romans 7:5-6 provides the key. For those who are "in the flesh," an encounter with the law rouses "the passions of sins," leading to acts of rebellion and death. The demands that incite such rebellion can hardly be exclusively ceremonial; on the contrary, the example Paul provides in verse 7 is the (moral) prohibition of coveting. Yet in the preceding verse Paul says that believers have been "set free from the law"

49. Galatians 3:19, 23-25; see 2 Corinthians 3:11, 14. Romans 10:4 makes the same point if Paul here means by the Greek word *telos* "end" and not simply "goal."

50. Romans 7:6; Galatians 2:19.

51. Romans 7:6.

52. Romans 6:14-15.

53. Galatians 4:5.

54. See Romans 8:4; 13:8-10; Galatians 5:14.

55. Note esp. Romans 2:14-27.

56. Everyone, of course, concedes that Paul also means that Christians have been delivered from the curse that follows transgression of the law. See Galatians 3:13.

(the context forbids us to limit the latter statement to the law's ritual aspects), so that they now serve God "in the new way of the spirit and not the old way of the letter."

Note that there is no question (could there ever be?) that Christians are obligated to serve God. Nor is there (for Paul) any question that believers, as dwellers in God's world, are subject to precisely the same universal obligations of truth, goodness, and love that are spelled out in the moral demands of the Mosaic law. Indeed, when they live as they ought and as they are enabled by the divine spirit that indwells them, their conduct will prove unexceptionable by the standards of the law.[57] They will, in effect, have "fulfilled" the law.[58] Paul's point is rather that believers do not encounter these obligations as *law*.

"Law," in this Pauline usage, stands not simply for the concrete commands and prohibitions found in Torah, but also for the mode in which these obligations encounter rebellious humanity "in the flesh": as commands that are externally imposed (their inscription on tablets of stone is in marked contrast with demands recognized and endorsed within human hearts)[59] upon a will bent on its self-assertion. The Mosaic law in all of its parts — moral as well as ritual commandments, sanctions as well as demands — was intended for a favored people who are nonetheless representative of humanity "in the flesh." Among them it could only exacerbate — while it defined and condemned — humanity's rebellion.[60] For a humanity being prepared for restoration to its intended place in God's creation, for a humanity (as Paul puts it) that has yet to "come of age,"[61] God provided a fitting and graphic reminder in his covenant with Israel that he is good, that human beings have been made to enjoy fellowship with him, and that that fellowship requires their own submission to the good. Inevitably, the latter requirement could only encounter Adamic humanity as *law*.

But law (in this sense) is a matter of the past for a humanity that has "come of age." Its ceremonial aspects were never intended for any

---

57. Galatians 5:22-23.

58. Romans 8:4; 13:8-10; Galatians 5:14.

59. 2 Corinthians 3:3, 7; cf. Jeremiah 31:31-34. Like Romans 7:6, 2 Corinthians 3:6 contrasts service enjoined by the "letter" with that driven by the indwelling divine spirit.

60. Note how Paul links the spheres of the Mosaic "law" and the "flesh" in Romans 7:5-6, 14-24; Galatians 3:2-3; Philippians 3:3-4 together with verse 9.

61. Galatians 3:23-26; 4:1-7.

but Jews. But even its moral demands now have a different character. To be sure, murder, adultery, and theft are as wrong for Christians as they ever were for Israel "under the law." Moreover, so long as Christians are subject to the weakness and temptations of life in a sin-scarred world, they will need guidance (or, at the least, reminders) about which kinds of behavior are appropriate and which kinds are inappropriate and wrong for them to show as the redeemed people of God. We may go further. There is, in Paul's understanding, a continuing place for figures of authority in the church to provide such guidance and, if necessary, to insist upon its obligatory nature. Paul himself does not hesitate to advise, to remind, to command. But even where he commands, he insists that he is merely spelling out what is implicit in his Christian readers' own faith and experience of God.[62] Appropriate behavior for believers is, for Paul, the natural expression of their trust in God and their experience of his indwelling spirit.[63] They have "crucified the flesh";[64] no longer, then, can God's will confront them as an arbitrary, vexing, and provocative *law*.

62. See Romans 15:14-15; 1 Thessalonians 4:9-10.
63. Galatians 5:6, 22-23.
64. Galatians 5:24; cf. Romans 8:9.

Chapter 10

At Home in the Cosmos

ROMANS 8:14-39

The Root of All Evil

IT IS, *they* say, a dog-eat-dog world; in living by their creed, *they* lend it credibility.

Such a creed, and such a world, can see no virtue in loyalty, kindness, courage, or truth;[1] nor can these latter have opposing vices. Trust is naïveté. *Distrust* — in any and every relationship — is essential to the goal of being numbered with the devourers rather than the devoured. Society may impose constraints upon the conduct of its members to maximize and protect their perceived self-interests; but apart from such contracts, morality has no force. Nor is there any obvious basis for condemning those who succeed in flaunting society's norms. On the contrary, on such a view, the lifestyle of those who assert their own will at the expense of others is most in tune with the nature of reality. Still, not even tyrants can feel "at home" in such a cosmos: sooner or later, they too will be its victims.

In the "Jewish-Christian" vision[2] of reality, there is goodness at the foundation of the cosmos, the source of its existence, order, and life. Consequently, an obligation to goodness rests upon all moral

---

1. Indeed, such a vision of reality may well be thought to foster a "hermeneutic of suspicion" that dismisses all claims to virtue (which it cannot recognize) as screens for self-interest (which it descries everywhere).

2. For the sense in which I use the phrase, see Chapter One, n. 7.

beings: an obligation to trust, to affirm, and to pattern their lives according to the goodness at the source of their being. Moral codes may be of human construction. But the obligations of morality that such codes encapsulate (with limited and widely varied success) are given with the order of the cosmos. The obligations may be embraced or defied. Their defiance may, among human beings, be universal.[3] They are not for that reason subject to change. Truth is good. Loyalty is good. Kindness is good. Courage in pursuing any of these goods is itself good. And "good" cannot here be reduced to the "pleasant" or the "useful," since there are times when the pursuit of such goods is neither pleasant nor obviously useful: yet they remain good,[4] and it is the duty of moral beings, in a universe built upon goodness, to embrace them.

Conversely, there can be evil in such a cosmos. Unless there is in the cosmos an inherent goodness binding upon humans and not of their own devising, "evil" can mean nothing worse than "causing unpleasant sensations" or "hurtful to goals defined by human beings." Even the most heinous of human atrocities and the most devastating of "natural" disasters can hardly be *evil* in any more significant sense than "not to our liking" unless we can say why they ought not to be. Such an "ought," it seems, can only be found in a cosmos that is ultimately good — where there is inherent rightness in all that affirms and inherent evil in whatever disrupts and defies the good. The "problem of evil" can exist only in a world where "goodness" and "evil" have a reality transcending human preference, and where goodness is fundamental.

Evil is most emphatically a problem in the "Jewish-Christian" world. The abuse and murder of a child, the callous beating of the elderly in order to steal their pocket-change, the atrocities of war: these things, the "Jewish-Christian" vision of the world insists, are more than dis-

---

3. On this vision of reality (particularly in its Pauline form, marked by its perception of radical evil), many of the claims made by the various "hermeneutics of suspicion" can be allowed to be true: lamentably, self-interest *does* masquerade as virtue. The difference from the cynicism of "dog-eat-dog" hermeneutics lies partly in the adverb, partly in the absence of an ideological need to posit self-interest as the motivating force behind *all* of the activities of *all* of the Mother Theresas of the world.

4. One thinks, e.g., of characters in Solzhenitsyn novels who refuse to comply with official deceit at incredible personal cost. The depictions were not the product of authorial fantasy.

tasteful. They are evil. They ought not to be. Nor, for that matter, are things as they ought when I strike my child in anger, slander a rival, lust for what is not mine, neglect the needy at my doorstep. Such vices may be common, and commonly excused. In the "Jewish-Christian" world they remain wrong, a distortion of what my life and the world were meant to be.

There would be no evil — on such a view — if the creatures whom God has endowed with the capacity for moral goodness had maintained faith in him. One can be "at home" in the "Jewish-Christian" cosmos: cared for and reliant upon God's goodness. Were I to trust divine goodness as I ought, I would not be tempted to lie, to cheat, to covet, to steal, to hurt, to become jealous or bitter. The temptations result from my failure to trust, my will to choose and fend for myself, my growing awareness that much is beyond my control, my attempts to control things nonetheless, the inevitable fears and frustrations bred by my insistence on doing the immoral and the impossible. A vicious cycle of evil has been initiated by my failure to keep faith, by my will — in defiance of the obvious truth of my dependence upon God — to rule my own destiny and redefine "good" and "evil" to my liking.

The Overcoming of Evil

In the "Jewish-Christian" vision, evil springs from bad faith toward an already existing good. By the same vision, evil cannot survive forever. God, who is good, must oppose evil, overcome it, and — so *creative* is God's goodness — provide in the process redemption for his fallen creatures. Such is the biblical script where goodness is seen as foundational, but evil is nonetheless real.

In the Christian vision of the apostle Paul, God intervenes in the person of his son, who lives the life of perfect trust and obedience that all were made to enjoy. All have not done so, however; and when God's son takes upon himself the lot of Adamic humanity, he bears the brunt of its wickedness. He does so willingly, however, out of love for sinners.[5]

5. 2 Corinthians 5:14; Galatians 2:20.

In so doing, by the Father's will, he provides atonement for sin: through his death the bane of sin is exhausted.[6] His resurrection to new life establishes the divine approval of his self-sacrifice,[7] his restoration to divine glory,[8] the divinely offered possibility of a new life — with Christ — lived in God's service,[9] and the hope that the One who raised Christ from the dead will one day do the same for Christ's adopted "brothers."[10] Such is the divine salvation offered in Paul's "gospel": divine in its confounding of human horizons,[11] in its unqualified abhorrence of sin,[12] in the sheer selflessness of its love,[13] in its power to overcome sin and death.[14]

Sin and death — Paul declares — have been conquered. But before they are eradicated forever, humanity's faith in God must be restored through the proclamation of the gospel; otherwise the inevitable purging of creation from all that disrupts its goodness must wipe away humanity as well.[15] "Now is the time when God extends his favor; now is the day of salvation."[16] For a time, then, even those who belong to the new humanity "in Christ" must continue in conditions determined by sin: in bodies that are mortal, subject to deprivation, temptation, persecution.[17] Of their coming salvation they enjoy for the present only a foretaste: the gift of the indwelling Spirit, making real the presence and love of God.[18] Otherwise their deliverance is a matter of hope that is not yet seen, of a yearning — shared by all creation — for liberation from the corruption and havoc of sin. The life of the age to come may be incredibly blessed; but, for the moment, it is only in its birth pangs.[19]

6. Romans 3:25-26.
7. See Romans 4:24-25.
8. Philippians 2:5-11; Romans 8:34.
9. Romans 6:4, 8-11.
10. Romans 8:11, 29.
11. 1 Corinthians 1:18-25.
12. Romans 8:3.
13. Romans 5:8; Galatians 2:20.
14. Romans 8:3-4, 11; 1 Corinthians 15:54-57.
15. See 1 Thessalonians 1:9-10.
16. 2 Corinthians 6:2.
17. Romans 8:10, 23; 2 Corinthians 4:7-12.
18. Romans 8:23; cf. Romans 5:5 and 8:15-16.
19. Romans 8:19-25.

And there is a fittingness in that. God's son suffered the brunt of human evil because of his love for human beings; surely, Paul feels, people should count it a privilege if they in turn are allowed to suffer for his sake,[20] to be granted a share in his suffering.[21] Such suffering (Paul assures his readers), however severe (and Paul's own experience belongs in this category),[22] is nothing in comparison with the glory in store for those who love God.[23] They are, moreover, sustained in every circumstance by an overwhelming sense of God's love.

In every circumstance: Paul does his best to list them all.[24] In the process he mentions not only physical deprivation and hardship, danger, opposition, and death, but also whatever supernatural powers there may be ("angels and rulers . . . and powers") that are malevolently disposed toward God's people. Although this is the only mention of such powers in the whole argument of Romans,[25] we can hardly conclude that Paul did not take them seriously. Undoubtedly he did, as others who share his "vision" have always done. There is no apparent reason why humans should be the only moral beings created by a God of goodness. Still, God, the Source and Sustainer of all life, is, ultimately, the only One with whom his creatures have to deal. No malevolent power is needed to explain human sin.[26] No force hostile to God can prevent his salvific work.[27] None can drive a wedge between God's people and God's love.[28] Powers of darkness are mentioned only to be dismissed as forces to be reckoned with.

In Paul's vision, encounters with distress, hunger, danger, and death cannot, in the end, determine human destiny. The decisive confrontation must be with divine love. It surrounds, sustains, embraces

20. Philippians 1:29; cf. Romans 8:36; Galatians 6:17.
21. Romans 8:17; 2 Corinthians 4:7-12; Philippians 3:10.
22. 2 Corinthians 11:23-30.
23. Romans 8:18; 2 Corinthians 4:17.
24. Romans 8:35-39.
25. Unless we allow that Paul, in personifying "sin" in passages such as Romans 5:12, 21 and 6:12, has a more personal power (like Satan) in mind. The personification is not carried through with sufficient consistency, however, to make such a reading likely. Assurance that Satan will eventually be overcome is given in Romans 16:20.
26. See Romans 1:18–3:20.
27. See Romans 8:33-34.
28. Romans 8:35-39.

all. It offers all a home.[29] Those who respond in faith are adopted into God's family and know him as their *father*.[30]

The early Christian emphasis on God as Father derives from the centrality of the theme in Jesus' own teaching.[31] The title, of course, presupposes that God is the source of all life. It presupposes as well his authority, and the duty of his children to submit to the Father's will.[32] Paul introduces yet a further motif to the fatherhood theme when he declares that God's children will inherit — as God's "heirs" — what God has set aside for their eternal enjoyment.[33]

But the primary note is that of childlike trust in a benevolent father.[34] Ultimately, it is only with God that his creatures have to deal,

29. Paul's language of "election" will concern us in the next chapter. The universal scope of God's love and redemptive plan is, for Paul, beyond question. See, e.g., 2 Corinthians 5:14-15, 19; Romans 11:32.

30. Romans 8:14-17.

31. Hence the preservation, in the midst of Paul's Greek text, of the Aramaic "Abba" used by his Lord (Romans 8:15; also Galatians 4:6). Cf. Mark 14:36; and, on the theme, Matthew 5:43-48; 6:7-9, 32; 7:11.

32. 1 Corinthians 15:24-28; Mark 14:36; John 12:49-50; 14:28, 31; Hebrews 12:5-11. See the discussion of authority in the section "Notions of Freedom" in Chapter Eight above.

33. Romans 8:17; Galatians 4:7.

34. It is tragic — on a host of levels — that the family experience of some does not lead them to link goodness and trust with the father-child relationship; in the early Christian language of God as Father, the association is instinctive and unquestioned (Romans 8:15; Matthew 7:11). *Maternal* solicitude was of course proverbial for the biblical writers, and offered a ready comparison (seldom exploited, however; but see Isaiah 49:15; 66:13) to divine care. It is nonetheless true that God is not spoken of, or addressed, as "Mother" in the biblical texts, though frequently as "Father." It does not follow that the writers of the Bible thought God to be (sexually differentiated as) male. The language of sexual differentiation, of "male and female," is applied to *created* species and linked (perspicaciously!) to their propagation (Genesis 1:27-28). Such language is not used of God, nor are divine creative acts thought of as sexual (not even the impregnation of Mary, who bears God's son, is portrayed as the result of a sexual encounter). On the other hand, God was no doubt "thought of" as "male" in a more limited sense: the divine being was believed to demonstrate personal will and activity, and humans naturally "think of" (and speak of) a personal being in male or female terms — not both or neither. If one may speculate why the (masculine) language of Fatherhood was deemed the more appropriate, the answer may lie in part in that the male was thought in antiquity to be *generative* of new life, which the female merely bore; and, in part, in that "Fatherhood" was more suggestive of the *authority* believed to be appropriately and benevolently exercised by the Creator of all life.

Again, the mention of "authority" requires the reminder that ancient horizons and his children need not approach him with fear. The gift of God's spirit assures them of his love and enables them to address him with confidence: "Abba! Father!" Whatever may be their lot in a sin-scarred world, God's power and goodness guarantee that, in the end, "all things" will be seen to have "worked together" for their good.[35]

---

differed from our own. If (as many today are wont to claim) all human good is self-defined, it may well seem to follow that all should be free to define and pursue their *own* goals and paths to self-fulfillment. If, on the other hand, as the "Jewish-Christian" vision maintains, human beings are subject to universal demands of goodness, truth, and love, then authority exercised in keeping with these demands is far from problem-atic: mutual commitment to common goals can allow the exercise of, and submission to, such authority as providing the framework of a relationship of mutual love. (See, e.g., John 5:19-23; 6:38; 8:28-29; 14:31; 15:9; Ephesians 5:21-31; Hebrews 13:17; 1 Peter 5:1-5. That authority can be abused for the selfish ends of those who wield it was, of course, also recognized and the subject of frequent warnings: Ezekiel 34:1-10; Ephesians 6:4; 1 Peter 5:2-3, and elsewhere.) Those who view the world in the former way are liable to regard the structures of authority inherent in the latter as arbitrary and restric-tive, if not oppressive. Those who view things in the latter way are liable to see the competitive individualism and the individualistic, self-centered ideals of fulfillment characteristic of much modern thinking as introducing a tentativeness and instability into human relations that prevent people from maturing in mutual trust and committed love. Whether or not the two ideals can (or should) be combined lies beyond the purpose of the present study to explore. It should at least be said that those who would reproduce the New Testament today devoid of its language of authority run the risk of confusing Pauline ideals of freedom with what Paul considers humanity's fundamental sin: the declaration of human autonomy and the prioritizing of self-rule over the rightful claims of truth, goodness, and love. As we have repeatedly seen, freedom of choice is the *highest* ideal only in a very different vision of reality from that of "Jewish-Christian" faith.

35. Romans 8:28.

Chapter 11

The Triumph of God in History

ROMANS 9:1–11:36

MEANWHILE, what has become of Israel?

If only as an academic question, the issue was bound to arise for Paul. Adamic humanity, as we have seen, is made up (for Paul) of creatures of God dependent upon him and determined not to admit it; among them God chose Israel to serve as a model and reminder of his universal rule. Himself a Jew, Paul needed no rehearsal to list the prerogatives ascribed to his people: they had been adopted as God's children; had known the "glory" — the sensed and awesome presence of God; had entered covenants with God that spelled out how they might continue to enjoy his blessing; had been granted God's law, a sanctuary where they could approach and worship him, and promises of future favors. Their forebears included men who had walked with God, and it was in their midst that Messiah had been born. Truly God had been good to Israel.[1]

Still, for all of God's goodness to Israel, Adamic humanity remained estranged from him. None of these favors, Paul believed, had fundamentally altered Israel's own sinful bent, still less that of the pagan nations. God demonstrated his *tzedakah* — his faithfulness and goodness toward his creation — decisively and triumphantly in Jesus Christ, providing atonement for all of humanity's sins, deliverance from its bondage to sin and death, and reconciliation to himself. The proclamation of the gospel created both the need for and the possibility of a response of faith in God.

The problem that Paul faces in Romans 9–11 is that Israel itself

---

1. Romans 9:4-5.

101

has not responded with the faith essential for salvation.[2] Does this mean that God's promises to Israel will go unfulfilled? That God's plan for humanity's redemption has met ironic frustration in the unbelief of his own erstwhile people?

This possibility is summarily dismissed.[3] Still, Israel's place in the divine scheme remains a quandary to be explored. And for Paul it is far from academic. His personal engagement with the fate of his people, his grief that they — though peculiarly favored — should prove so resistant to God's offered salvation, the conviction in his bones that God's goodness and redemptive purpose will nonetheless prevail even in the case of Israel: all require that he dedicate extended treatment to the theme. In considering the main lines of his argument, we will look, first, at how Paul views the condition of his Jewish contemporaries in relation to the divine agenda; second, at what he believes Israel's future to be; and third, at the place in his argument of human responsibility on the one hand and the overarching divine will on the other.

God and Israel's Unbelief

(1) Israel's lack of faith, though a source of anguish for Paul,[4] can hardly (he believes) represent a breakdown in God's plan, since that plan never entailed the inclusion of every descendant of Abraham in the community of blessing.[5] (2) Indeed, God himself is active, and achieving his purposes, in the unbelief of Jews as well as in the coming to faith of Gentiles hitherto excluded from his people.[6] (3) Israel, of course, is active as well. In their case Paul perceives a misguided adherence to the law and its "works" that keeps them from submitting, in faith, to the divine *tzedakah*[7] demonstrated in Christ. As a result, Israel turns a deaf ear to the proclamation of the gospel.[8] (4) Yet, while much of Israel

2. Note Romans 10:1.
3. Romans 9:6. Cf. Romans 11:1, 11.
4. Romans 9:1-3; 10:1.
5. So Romans 9:6-13 argues.
6. So Paul argues in Romans 9:14-29.
7. On the term, see the discussion in Chapter Two above.
8. So Romans 9:30–10:21.

remains as wayward as ever, a minority (or "remnant") has believed; and there is both precedent and prophetic sanction for the perpetuation of God's relations with his covenant people through a tiny segment of their number.[9]

1. The unbelief prevailing among his Jewish contemporaries does not, for Paul, imply that God's commitment to his people has been frustrated. Nothing is new, Paul insists, in the current situation. The Israel that has enjoyed God's favor has, from its inception, been made up of a *selection* from among Abraham's descendants: Isaac, not Ishmael; Jacob, not Esau. Not physical descent from Abraham, but the divine promise is what effectively constitutes the community of blessing; hence, though divine promises were given to Abraham's offspring, God is free to select the objects of the promise from among those descendants. Provided *some* Jews find seats in the pews of the church, God's promise is not called in question by the conspicuous absence of their compatriots.

2. Paul is prepared to go further. Far from frustrating God, Israel's unbelief represents an integral part of the divine purpose: God himself has "hardened" their hearts.[10] Paul postpones until Romans 11 his discussion of what God means to achieve in the process. For the moment, he is content to insist that hardening people's hearts falls well within the prerogatives of their Creator: Has not the potter the right to turn one lump of clay into a decorative vase, another into a pot that is merely functional?

An understanding of Paul's claims at this point is frequently hampered by the penchant of interpreters to isolate the verses from all that "has gone before" in the argument of Romans, all that "is now" in the immediate context, and all that later "shall be" in Paul's development of the theme in Romans 11. Forgetting that Paul's talk of divine hardening, in the immediate context, must refer to Israel's resistance to the gospel, interpreters have understood Paul as saying that all who have ever failed to believe have had their hearts hardened by God. Forgetting that Paul has just devoted substantial parts of eight chapters to a depiction of Adamic humanity as alienated from God by its own refusal to

9. So we may summarize Romans 11:1-10.

10. The notion is, of course, a traditional one. See Isaiah 6:9-10; Mark 4:11-12; John 12:37-40.

acknowledge and submit to his goodness, interpreters have portrayed the objects of divine hardening as innocent human beings who have been *made* sinners — by the hardening activity of God! Forgetting that Paul will later explain the hardening of sinners as a temporary divine measure intended to bring salvation to all the peoples of the earth, interpreters have suggested that Paul thinks God hardens the hearts of otherwise innocent individuals in order to damn them forever (while, to be sure, predestining other individuals for salvation). To their credit, at least some of the interpreters who so isolate and construe Romans 9 concede that the chapter is not very representative of Paul's thought!

We need to retrace our steps. *Presupposed* throughout Romans 9–11 is the estrangement of Adamic humanity from God;[11] Paul proposes to disclose something of the mysterious way in which, in the course of history, God operates to reconcile the earth's peoples to himself. Paul never attributes humanity's bent toward sin to divine action. He does, however, claim (with ample precedent in the Hebrew Scriptures) that God can, when the need arises, channel human hostility to what is good into particular acts that promote his own purposes.[12] The upshot of this way of thinking is that either God *or* the people acting

---

11. This presupposition must be kept in mind when we read how, before they were even born, Isaac and Jacob were chosen as objects of the divine promise, while Ishmael and Esau were excluded (Romans 9:6-13); for Paul, Isaac *and* Ishmael, Jacob *and* Esau must inevitably be part of that sinful humanity whose redemption represents the ultimate goal of all of God's promises. In the immediate sequel, Paul's concern is to insist on God's prerogative to predetermine the role, whether honorable or dishonorable, played by his creatures in his plan. In Romans 11, however, Paul stresses that God's former "calling" of Israel (including Isaac and Jacob) as the community of his blessing and excluding of others (among whom must be reckoned Ishmael and Esau), as well as his present "calling" of Gentiles and hardening of Israel, both represent parts of a strategic plan whose purpose is the salvation of all the peoples of the earth (Romans 11:30-32).

12. In the Hebrew Scriptures divine judgment of evil — itself regarded as a good thing — is at times God's stated purpose in channeling existing human hostility into particular sins: so, most notably, Isaiah 6:9-13. A comparable case is found in 2 Thessalonians 2:10-12 (note, however, that the Pauline authorship of 2 Thessalonians is disputed by some scholars). Romans 1:24-32 has been interpreted along similar lines: God has channeled the energies of human beings who refuse to acknowledge him into deeds whose ugliness and viciousness effect their own punishment. On the other hand, Paul's language (God "gave them up" to such deeds) is perhaps more consistent with the view that God simply left sinners to follow the path of their own sins: a path leading inevitably to disaster.

can be seen as the agent of the activity in question: people, because their actions are consistent with, and expressive of, their rebellion against God's goodness; and God, because he has channeled that rebellion into specific acts that further his ends.

Thus the Pharaoh whose heart God hardened[13] was already the oppressor of God's people: but whereas ordinary prudence might have induced even his heart to release Israel prior to their decisive redemption,[14] God "hardened his heart" so that Israel — and "all the earth" — might witness what a holy arm, laid bare, could accomplish.[15] The pattern is found elsewhere as well. When Joseph's brothers sold him into slavery, they were clearly giving vent to their own hatred;[16] but God channeled that hatred (which could have been expressed in other, less productive ways, including murder) into an action that served his own intention to sustain his people through an imminent famine.[17] When God made Samson's love of a Philistine woman a part of his divine plan, he was hardly forcing Samson to act out of character.[18] The same is true, presumably, of the rashness of Rehoboam that effected God's intention to split the Israelite kingdom.[19] Paul explains Israel's present failure to respond to the gospel along similar lines.

---

13. Exodus 4:21; 7:3-5. But note that, in other texts, Pharaoh is said to harden his own heart (Exodus 8:15, 32). God's "hardening," we may say, does not turn sheep into donkeys; it merely ensures that donkeys do their kicking at a divine cue. As a result, a kick on cue can be attributed with equal propriety to the willfulness of the beast or the wisdom of the Cue-giver. And Pharaoh remains responsible for the sin of his hardened heart (Exodus 9:34).

14. Note Exodus 10:7.

15. Exodus 7:3-5; 9:15-16; 10:1-2; Deuteronomy 7:17-19. Sinners — such as Pharaoh — are "ready for destruction" in any case: God could appropriately destroy them at once. God is, then, entirely within his rights when he chooses instead to preserve the life of people like Pharaoh so that they can serve as object lessons: on them God can demonstrate his own hostility to sin, his overwhelming power, and the splendor of his presence when he saves his people. So Romans 9:22-23, essentially paraphrasing Exodus 9:15-16. The point of the verses is not to spell out the ultimate destiny of those "fit for destruction" whom God preserves as object lessons, nor how they came to be so fitted; these issues are not even addressed. Paul's concern is rather to explain how God can use such people for his purposes and to insist on his right to do so.

16. Genesis 37:4, 18-28.

17. Genesis 45:5-8; 50:20.

18. Judges 14:1-4.

19. 1 Kings 12:15. The author of the book of Acts explains the crucifixion of Jesus

3. Thus, though on one level Israel's current unbelief represents an outworking of God's purposes (to be explored in Romans 11), on another it represents a fresh expression of the people's perennial resistance against God, for which they remain responsible. At this point Paul interrupts his discussion of the divine program in history to outline his understanding of how Israel, in this instance, has gone astray.

Since Adamic humanity is characterized (for Paul) by its refusal to acknowledge God and submit to his will, Adamic human beings can experience God's favor only if it is bestowed gratuitously by God, acting completely on his own initiative. God's blessing *cannot* be a divine response to God-pleasing activities of people incapable of pleasing God. This point is central to Paul's argument throughout these chapters. Isaac and Jacob, he has already insisted, were designated as the objects of divine favor before they were even born, before they had done anything good or bad. The initiative, then, was manifestly God's: God was "calling" those whom he chose to be his people without regard for their "works."[20] Furthermore, when God told Moses that he would show mercy to those on whom he had mercy, he again made it clear that the bestowing of his favor owed nothing to the will or activity of its objects.[21]

When, then, Paul goes on to say that Gentiles who have not pursued divine approval have nonetheless found such approval by faith,[22] the paradox is meant to draw attention to yet another instance of God's way of dealing with his sinful creatures: his favor has again been granted, not in response to human activity (the Gentiles were not active in seeking God's favor), but as a gift. Those who receive it as a gift are thereby moved to respond with faith: with trust, that is, in God's initiative of grace and goodness. But Israel, Paul claims, has not yet grasped this basic principle of faith; rather, they are seeking to secure God's favor with "works" of their own in conformity with his law.

---

in similar terms: Jesus was betrayed by a people who had always opposed and persecuted God's servants (Acts 7:51-52), and executed by soldiers who were themselves "lawless" (Acts 2:23); the latter, in turn, were acting at the behest of two of those "kings of the earth" who have always opposed God and his Anointed (Acts 4:25-27). Yet in all of these acts, each expressing the character of the actors, the predetermined plan of God was being accomplished (Acts 2:23; 4:26-28).

20. Romans 9:7-13.

21. Romans 9:15-16.

22. Romans 9:30.

Confronted by the decisive demonstration of God's *tzedakah* (his commitment to the good of his creation) in Christ Jesus, they have stumbled,
for their eyes were fixed on the *tzedakah* of an earlier divine revelation:
that of the Mosaic law.

The law, to be sure, was itself a gift of God's goodness, a reminder
of God's rule and of the demands it places upon his creatures. But Paul
is convinced that it did not — and could not — bring Adamic human
beings to trust and obey God as they ought. The atonement of humanity's sins, and the transformation of its rebellious bent into one of
submission to God, is effected only in Christ Jesus. With his coming,
the law has fulfilled its divinely intended, though limited, function. Jews
who reject the gospel while pursuing the law are credited with zeal; but
the zeal, Paul claims, is misplaced.[23] In the end, the Jews of his day are
proving — like their forebears — resistant to the purposes of God.[24]

4. Yet some Jews *have* believed: Paul himself is among them. In
fact, the contemporary situation, in Paul's mind, has close parallels from
the time of Elijah[25] and that of Isaiah:[26] in all three cases the existence
of a minority — a "remnant" — chosen by God's grace is sufficient
evidence of God's continued commitment to Israel.

The favored status of these few, Paul again insists, is the result of
divine grace, not of their human "works."[27] That the few must come to
faith does not, for Paul, negate this claim. Human faith, in his view, is
necessarily a *response* evoked by the proclamation of God's grace in
salvation.[28] And the response itself is made possible only when God,
the Creator of all light, illumines the hearts of his creatures: then they
see the presence of God in the person and work of Jesus Christ.[29] Those
who believe thus know themselves to be "chosen" and "called" by God's
grace. They are like clay fashioned by the divine Potter into objects of
beauty and honor. Those whose hearts are now hardened, on the other

23. Romans 10:2.
24. The autobiographical element in Paul's depiction of Jews "zealous" for the
law but hostile to the gospel — and hence to the purposes of God — should not be
forgotten. See Galatians 1:11-16.
25. Romans 11:2-6.
26. Romans 9:27-29.
27. Romans 11:5-6.
28. See Romans 10:17; 1 Corinthians 2:4-5; 15:11, 14; Galatians 3:2, 5.
29. 2 Corinthians 4:6; Galatians 1:15-16.

hand, are like clay fashioned for less honorable use.[30] It does not follow, however, that the latter are destined to be destroyed.[31]

God and the Future of Israel

Israel's prophetic tradition is dominated by denunciations of Israel's sins and warnings of pending doom; still, the notion that judgment could represent the *final* stage of God's dealings with his people proved unthinkable. Israel's ultimate restoration to divine favor is a recurrent theme. So, too, is the insistence that the restoration owes nothing to the character or deeds of an intractable people and everything to the will of the God who restores them.[32]

Paul sees Israel's future in similar terms. At the moment, their hearts are hardened while non-Jews are given the opportunity to hear and to respond to the gospel.[33] But the hardening — and the attendant rejection of the gospel — is not permanent: when God's appointed time has come, Israel's Redeemer will banish its "impiety"[34] and "unbelief";[35] Israel's "enmity" and "disobedience" toward the gospel[36] will give way to the obedience of faith, and so "all Israel will be saved."[37] In redeeming Adamic humanity, God proceeds by dividing and conquering the nations. For a time, the disobedience of Gentiles excluded them from God's favor while Jews were treated with mercy. Now Israel's disobedience — or, from

30. Romans 9:21; 11:7-10.
31. See Romans 11:11-32, and the discussion below.
32. See Ezekiel 20:5-44; 36:16-32; also 16:53-63; Isaiah 43:22–44:5; Micah 7:18-20. And note Psalm 79:8-9; Daniel 9:4-19.
33. Paul does not spell out why Israel's unbelief is necessary if Gentiles are to be given the opportunity to believe. Perhaps he recalls that the Christian mission turned to Gentiles only after Jews proved resistant. Or his thinking may be steered by the conviction — common in his day — that God's kingdom will come when the Jews submit to God's will (note Acts 3:19-20): hence the need that Gentiles first be given an opportunity to believe. In any case Paul sees the scheme of history that he outlines in Romans 11 adumbrated in Deuteronomy 32:21 (see Romans 10:19; 11:11, 14).
34. Romans 11:26.
35. Romans 11:20, 23.
36. Romans 11:28, 31.
37. Romans 11:26.

another perspective, the partial, temporary, strategic hardening of their hearts by God — gives Gentiles the opportunity to believe. "God has consigned all to disobedience, in order that he may show mercy to all."[38]

Does Paul mean that every Gentile and Jew will be saved? His words are certainly patient of such an interpretation;[39] still, it probably goes beyond his intentions. Throughout the passage, faith is a prerequisite of salvation; and though divine mercy is universal in its scope, Paul knows well that unbelief can persist.[40] Indeed, the grace of God can be "received to no purpose."[41] The claim that "all Israel" (or "Israel as a whole") will be "saved" is intended as a contrast to a situation in which a mere "remnant" has believed: it need not mean that every individual Israelite will in the end submit, in saving faith, to God.[42] And elsewhere, at least, Paul does speak of those who "are perishing."[43]

What is clear for Paul is that God has not abandoned creation to be destroyed by sin. He has extended his mercy to all of his creatures. In bringing salvation to all the peoples of the earth, he has seen fit to deal in favor now with one nation, now with another; he has excluded for a time the pagan nations, then hardened Israel's hearts in order that pagans might have the opportunity to believe. Paul's vision ends with the triumph of God's goodness among *all* nations, and gives way to praise of the divine wisdom.[44]

38. Romans 11:32.

39. Note also Romans 5:15-19; 1 Corinthians 15:22; and cf. Ephesians 1:9-10; Colossians 1:20.

40. Alternatively, the life of faith may be abandoned. Note the conditional force of Romans 11:22-23. Similarly 1 Corinthians 15:1-2; and note 1 Corinthians 9:26-27; 10:1-12. In each case, since divine benevolence is presupposed, the explicit condition upon which salvation depends involves the human response to God's goodness.

41. So 2 Corinthians 6:1. The whole passage (2 Corinthians 5:19–6:2) is instructive. God's purpose is to "reconcile the world to himself, not counting their transgressions against them." To Paul (and others) God has entrusted the task of communicating to the peoples of the world the divine offer of reconciliation: "We beg you, on Christ's behalf: Be reconciled to God!" The entreaty receives its urgency from the possibility of receiving, yet deriving no good from, the offer of God's grace ("Do not receive [the offer of] God's grace in vain!"). Hence the repeated appeal: "Now is the time when God will accept you, now is the day of salvation."

42. Cf. the allowance of exceptions at the time of Israel's restoration in Ezekiel 11:17-21; 20:38.

43. 1 Corinthians 1:18; 2 Corinthians 4:3; cf. Romans 2:5-10; Philippians 1:28.

44. Romans 11:33-36.

The Role of God in Human History

In these chapters Paul deals with issues bound to arise for those who adhere to the "Jewish-Christian" vision,[45] but to which that vision dictates no answer. His own focus is on Israel's resistance to the gospel. But human resistance to God's will takes many forms, and the relation between God's governance of his creation and the existence within that creation of that which (on some level at least) must be seen as *contrary* to his will must appear problematic to any who would think through the implications of Jewish or Christian faith. In what follows I will briefly sketch several possible answers before suggesting, in only slightly greater detail, what appears to be the thinking of Paul.

1. If there is a before and after with God (as there undoubtedly is with his creatures), and if God plays no role in determining the decisions of human beings, then he may be thought to be ignorant of any particulars of the future that are dependent on the exercising of human will.[46] His plans, whenever they are dependent on the actions of moral beings, will at best be contingent:[47] God could not know that Adam would sin, though he could, presumably, prepare for such an eventuality. Being God, he has the power to intervene in history at any point and impose his rule, rewarding some and punishing others; in that sense, history remains under his control. Still, his participation in history's course is minimal. The advantage of this perspective is that God is most evidently free of responsibility for the evil that humans bring upon themselves. He does not influence their actions — or even *know* of them in advance.

2. If there is no before and after with God, he may be thought to *know* all that (from a human perspective) is yet to transpire without being said to *cause* it. As a spectator on a hill sees but does not determine what lies ahead for a traveler below, so God, from the vantage of eternity, can know all that lies ahead for humans without being the cause of its happening. Divine planning (if the term still has any meaning) is obviously facilitated by such knowledge: divine schemes need no longer

---

45. On my usage of the phrase, see Chapter One, n. 7.

46. Divine "omniscience" will then refer to God's knowledge of all that is logically knowable, which will not include future contingencies.

47. This is indeed suggested by the language of Jeremiah 18:1-10.

be contingent. And God can still be thought to bear no responsibility for evil that he did not cause, though it is clear on this understanding that he has (fore)knowledge of its occurrence. His *control* of history is still limited to points of direct divine intervention.

3. At the opposite extreme to the foregoing positions is the third view, by which God is thought to predetermine the activities of all of his creatures, who are no more than puppets in his hands. He prescribes in advance the good and bad actions of all human beings, their faith or unbelief, their salvation or damnation. Humans may still choose their own actions, but God will have so shaped their character and circumstances that their choices are effectively predetermined by him. Clearly divine planning can here encounter no obstruction. Can we still speak of divine goodness? God (on this understanding) creates people whom he first causes to sin, then punishes for what they have done. A positive construal of the procedure might suggest that it was intended to demonstrate that sin is a bad thing; the demonstration, in turn, might be considered one of the predetermined divine means of bringing about the predetermined faith of those predestined for salvation. Perhaps more difficult to account for on this view is the *sinfulness* of sin for which God himself is the effective cause.

4. Somewhere between the second and third perspectives is a fourth position that sees humans as freely choosing their own activities, but God's foreknowledge as permitting him to incorporate those activities into his own divine plans. God is now seen to be in full control of history, shaping it to his own ends; but people remain free and responsible for what they do. The logic that finds incompatible divine foreknowledge and human freedom must (on this view) fail from human inability to fathom the ways and resources of the Almighty.

And what of Paul's position? Any suggestions should be prefaced with the reminder that Paul nowhere explores these issues systematically; that, even in Romans 9–11, Paul touches upon God's governance of history only as it relates to a particular, pressing problem: Israel's failure to respond to the gospel. Still (what I take to be) common *mis*constructions of Paul's understanding of divine governance require that we spell out what can be known on the subject.

1. Paul clearly attributes foreknowledge to God.[48] He is thus not among those who maintain the first position summarized above.

---

48. See, e.g., Romans 1:1-2; 15:4; Galatians 1:15-16; 3:8.

2. Paul's language of divine election[49] and hardening rules out the second position (as well as the first): God's involvement in human activities, in these instances at least, goes beyond (fore)*knowledge* of decisions independently arrived at by human beings. Even the fourth position seems too weak a statement to account for God's acts in electing, or hardening, his creatures.

3. Does Paul think that God predetermines *all* human activities and choices (the third alternative above)? Some have so construed him. But the answer must be No.

In fact, Paul speaks of divine predetermination only in a few, limited contexts; in each case, he has special reasons for thinking such an explanation necessary. Adamic human beings, for Paul, *cannot* become God's people, or even respond to God's goodness in faith, unless God, acting on his own initiative, creates those possibilities; hence the need for the "election" of believers. That God had predetermined Paul's apostleship seemed obvious: how else would such an opponent of the gospel ever have become its servant?[50] On the other hand, the divine hardening of Israel, in addition to being a scriptural motif that Paul would not have questioned, explained for Paul how Israel's unbelief could be a temporary condition that would not, in the end, exclude Israel from God's salvation. Paul exploited the divine hardening of Pharaoh (again, a traditional motif) to explain God's hardening of Israel: in Pharaoh's case, a hostile ruler was made an object lesson of divine wrath and a key actor in the drama of Israel's redemption. Note that in all of these cases, human bondage and alienation from God are *presupposed* as conditions *requiring* God to predetermine certain human activities if he is to bring about salvation. It would be presumptuous to suggest, on the basis of these special cases, that Paul thought God had predetermined *all* human activity. It would, indeed, be perverse to use these cases, all illustrating God's salvific purpose for human beings, as the basis for a claim that God predetermined as well the *sin* that effected humanity's alienation from God.

And, in fact, Paul provides us with no justification for doing so. He speaks of the origin of humanity's bent toward sin frequently enough,[51] but never suggests a divine role in the calamity. Indeed, his

---

49. Romans 11:5, 7; cf. Romans 8:29.
50. Galatians 1:11-16.
51. Romans 1:20-21; 5:12-19; 1 Corinthians 15:21; 2 Corinthians 11:3.

flat declaration that humanity's sinfulness is inexcusable[52] would seem to exclude any thought of divine predetermination. Paul can speak of God "giving [people] over" to their sins, and of the appropriateness of the abandonment in view of their choice to refuse him recognition.[53] Again, the language would seem to rule out the possibility that Paul thought God himself was the source of human sinfulness.

4. On the other hand, it might well seem to follow that, if divine election is necessary for Adamic human beings to come to faith, then God must *not* have "elected" those who do not believe. God would still not be responsible for the sin that condemns them. And yet, by electing some to salvation (though they merit only condemnation) and *not* electing others (who also merit only condemnation), God would effectively be predetermining who is saved and who is not.

But though the implications may seem to follow, Paul does not appear to have drawn them. A number of Pauline texts speak of God's redemptive purposes as universal.[54] Statements of predestination to damnation are not to be found; nor does Paul's language of the divine "election" and "calling" of believers *require* the view that the unbelief and condemnation of others have been predetermined. A number of texts suggest that divine grace can be resisted, and even that the "called" members of the Christian community may prove faithless and be lost.[55] It is possible, then, that Paul believed that ultimately only those would be lost who *resisted* or *abandoned* the call of divine grace. It is possible, too, that (at times at least) he ventured to hope that *all*, one day, would be redeemed.[56]

In short, Paul clearly reckons with divine foreknowledge; he thinks that humanity bears full responsibility for its alienation from God and potential condemnation; he believes that God can, on occasion, channel human hostility to goodness into particular acts of sinfulness that further his purposes; he declares that God has chosen and "called" those who believe; he affirms that God's redemptive purposes are universal;

52. Romans 1:20; cf. Romans 3:19.

53. Romans 1:21-28.

54. Romans 5:15-19; 11:30-32; 1 Corinthians 15:22; 2 Corinthians 5:14-15, 19; and note (though the Pauline authorship of these letters is disputed) Ephesians 1:9-10; Colossians 1:20.

55. Romans 8:12-13; 11:22-23; 1 Corinthians 3:16-17; 9:26-27; 10:1-12; 15:1-2; 2 Corinthians 6:1; Galatians 5:2-4; 6:7-8; 1 Thessalonians 3:5.

56. See n. 43 above.

he suggests that God's grace and "call" can be resisted, to damning effect; and he is not unambivalent in statements whether or not there will, in the end, be any "lost."

Paul nowhere attempts to reduce his convictions in these matters to a logical system. He believes what appears to him to follow from God's demonstrated *tzedakah* in Christ Jesus, seen as the culmination of a divine plan that included both Abraham and Moses. Yet even that demonstration and that perceived design provide, not unambiguous answers to all conceivable questions, but only grounds sufficient for trusting the goodness and the wisdom — surpassing mortal understanding — of the Creator, Redeemer, and Judge of all humankind.

Chapter 12

On Living the Good Life

ROMANS 12:1–16:27

NOT INFREQUENTLY, I find myself confronted with a ballot containing a list of names I do not recognize, none of which I can even vaguely link with a face, an interest, or a policy. If I proceed to mark my ballot anyway, I will play a part in the election of my representative; but I can hardly be said to have "exercised my right to *choose* my representative," since no meaningful choice has been made. "Choice" implies preference. Faced with alternative courses of action, I *choose* the one that appears to me most satisfying, most likely to bring me closer to some goal I have set, most beneficial or pleasing to someone I love, most in keeping with principles I cherish. In each instance, something I *value* is expressed in my choice. Where this is not the case, where no judgment based on values that I hold is involved, I have not made a meaningful human "choice." The outcome could just as well have been determined by the flip of a coin.[1]

If genuine human choice can be exercised only on the basis of values people already hold, then our basic values themselves cannot be the product of genuine choice. In this respect, our values resemble

---

1. A special case merits mention here. Often I must decide between alternatives that express *competing* values that I do in fact hold: whether, for example, I will tell the truth or save my skin. I make a meaningful choice if I decide that one value is more important to me than the other and act upon that *preference*. If, on the other hand, I can see no basis for favoring one value above the other, and my decision is based on nothing more than the equivalent of a coin-toss, my choice is less than meaningful. In such a case, however, it does at least express the affirmation of a value that I hold.

our beliefs, or the trust we put in other people. I can choose to act (for any number of reasons) as *if* I believed a certain proposition, even though in reality I am not convinced of its truth; but I can truly *believe* only what I find believ*able*. (Put differently: I cannot truly be said to believe a statement that I find less than believable.) I can choose to act (for any number of reasons) as *if* I trusted the elderly man next door, even though I am not persuaded that he is reliable. I may, for example, lend him my lawnmower even though he lost my weedcutter, because I value good relations with my neighbor. But I can truly *trust* only those I deem to be trust*worthy*. (Put differently: I cannot truly be said to trust a person I think less than trustworthy — though I may act as though I did and hope for the best.) Similarly, I can choose to act (for any number of reasons, some quite cynical) as *if* I placed value on compassion, even though in reality I care for no one but myself; but I can truly *value* compassion only if I sense that compassion is *good.* (Put differently, I cannot truly be said to value compassion if I sense nothing good about it.) I cannot arbitrarily choose my values.[2]

One need not be able to spell out and defend one's values to live a focused, "principled" life: many do so instinctively. Some, indeed, live by values that they could not defend, since their values have no place within their own stated vision of reality. People may, for example, display in practice a keen sense that certain things are "right" (that is, that they *ought* to be done) while others are "wrong" (that is, they ought *not* to be done), even though, in theory, they dismiss such distinctions as arbitrary conventions.[3] More integrated personalities act on values that directly reflect their worldview (whether or not they themselves could show the linkage) and consistently allow those values to shape their behavior. If, in addition, they are able to communicate to others their vision of reality in a compelling way and convince them, as a result, to adopt principles of behavior consistent with their vision, they qualify as moral thinkers and teachers.

2. It follows that a life for which freedom of choice is the *only* value is devoid of meaning. That is, a "choice" between alternatives is meaningless unless I find something of value in the alternative chosen, and that value itself (as we have seen) cannot be chosen. Children in whom no value but self-determination is inculcated will be utterly unable to decide for themselves on a meaningful course of action.

3. See the discussion of "The Modern West and 'Sin'" in Chapter Three above.

The legacy of Paul for nearly two thousand years is that of a moral thinker of extraordinary impact. He was himself utterly enthralled by a vision of reality, and his captivation proved contagious. But he also succeeded in spelling out principles of behavior appropriate to that vision. To this point the vision itself has been the focus of this book. We conclude, as Paul concludes Romans, by noting briefly the principles of behavior that Paul derives from it.

Discussions of Pauline ethics tend to focus on the related issues of freedom and the law.[4] We may begin by observing that the notion of the *good* is more fundamental to his moral thought. A brief look at what he means by "the good" will follow, then a summary statement of how Paul envisages life in its service.

The Obligation of Goodness

The obligation to goodness is, in Paul's mind, universal; not so, however, the obligation to law.

1. In Romans 2, Paul repeatedly distinguishes between Jews, to whom the law was given and who are responsible for its observance, and Gentiles, who neither have nor will be judged by the law. Yet the criterion of judgment, he insists, is the same for both.

> God will give to all according to their deeds. To those who persist in doing *good* and so pursue the path that leads to glory, honor, and lasting blessedness, he will give eternal life. But for those who are self-seeking, who disobey the truth and obey what is wicked, wrath and anger are in store. Distress and anguish will come upon all who practise what is evil: Jews in the first place, but also Greeks. Glory, honor, and true prosperity will be the reward of all who practise what is *good*, Jews in the first place, but also Greeks. There is no prejudice with God.[5]

4. The Mosaic law is intended (as usually in Paul) by unqualified references to "the law."

5. Romans 2:6-11.

Jews and non-Jews alike must "practise what is good." God has, to be sure, favored Jews with a concrete statement of what the good requires — though that knowledge, Paul adds, is useless unless matched by behavior.[6] But Gentiles, though without the law, are subject to the same moral demands. Note the direction of Paul's thought. The good is not defined as that which God, in his law, commands; rather, the rule of God's law over the Jews is justified because the law spells out the universal demands of what is good.[7] Paul later claims that those who do no evil to their neighbors have thereby fulfilled the law.[8] Again, the presupposition is not that the commands of the law arbitrarily *define* what is good or evil, but that they *embody* the good; hence those who do what is good and avoid evil, whether or not they are familiar with the law, in fact fulfill the law's demands.[9]

In short, human obligation to the good is universal. The law of Moses is merely the form in which Jews encounter that obligation.

2. Indeed, Paul declares that sin was rampant before the law was even given.[10] The law brought definition to existing sin, increased its visibility, gave its condemnation "legal" grounds. But even without law, in the period between Adam and Moses, human beings were bound by an obligation to the good — which they defied.

3. Paul believes, moreover, that Christians have "died to the law."[11] Its hegemony he confines to humanity "in the flesh": to those insistent on self-rule and resistant to any demand that they acknowledge their dependence upon God and yield him appropriate praise. To rebellious human beings the law serves as a reminder of their creaturely limitations and obligations. Inevitably, it exacerbates their rebellion. From that way

---

6. Romans 2:17-24.

7. Note also the justification of the law in Romans 7:12. In the immediate sequel, Paul writes as one who wants to do the "good" but cannot (Romans 7:18-19, 21): again, the law is said to be good *because it corresponds* to the good that Paul acknowledges ought to be done (Romans 7:15-16).

8. Romans 13:10.

9. See also Romans 2:25-29. Excluded from consideration in both Romans 2 and Romans 7 are the laws which Paul, together with Jewish tradition, saw as binding only on Israel. See the discussion of "The Place of Law in Deuteronomy" in Chapter Four above.

10. Romans 5:12-14.

11. Romans 7:5-6; cf. Galatians 2:19.

of life, and from the law that provoked and condemned it, Christians have been set free.

But the obligation to goodness remains. Paul portrays the good life in Romans 12–16 with scarcely a mention of the law.[12] When he goes on to say that all foods may be eaten and that no day need be considered more sacred than any other,[13] he speaks in obvious disregard of much that the Mosaic law prescribes.[14] But Christians are still bound to do the good.

> Detest what is evil, cling to what is good.[15]

> Do not be overcome by evil, but overcome evil with good.[16]

> Do what is good, and you will receive praise from your rulers. For they are servants of God for your own well-being, promoting what is good. But if you do what is evil, you have cause to fear.[17]

> I want you to be wise when it comes to the good, innocent when it comes to evil.[18]

Ultimately, then, Paul's understanding of the "good life" is not determined by compliance with law; nor is it distinguished by limitless freedom. The mark of the good life is its orientation toward the "good."

12. He notes only (Romans 13:8-10) that those who live in love thereby fulfill what the law demands.

13. Romans 14:1-9, 14.

14. Though Paul believes, as we have seen, that the Mosaic law contains commands that embody the universal requirements of goodness, he also thinks that it includes other demands serving a more limited function among Jews (see n. 9 above). Christians, in his view, are *not* subject to the law since (1) the latter demands do not apply to them; (2) the former demands are not dependent on the law of Moses for their validity; and (3) the law was given to confront and condemn the rebellion of humanity "in the flesh."

15. Romans 12:9.

16. Romans 12:21.

17. Romans 13:3-4.

18. Romans 16:19.

The Definition of the Good

In none of these passages does Paul spell out his understanding of the "good." Still, its Pauline definition should (by this time!) be straightforward. Two ways in which Paul summarizes the Christian's moral responsibility provide the necessary clues.

1. In 1 Thessalonians 2:12, Paul urges his converts to behave in a manner "*worthy* of the God who calls [them] to his own kingdom and glory." Paul also challenged the Philippian Christians to conduct themselves in a way "*worthy* of the gospel of Christ."[19] The "good" life, then, involves a "worthy" or "appropriate" response to God's demonstrated goodness.

Moderns, intent on giving their world a shape that suits them, insist on their liberty to do so. Their highest good, we may say, is freedom. Paul would see such a notion of freedom as built upon illusions. People are born into a world they did not make, into relationships they did not choose; they are (he would maintain) dependent on God for every breath they take, every gift they possess. Those who refuse to acknowledge God or to give him thanks express something more than freedom by their actions: their behavior reflects a suppression of the truth, self-absorption, self-deception, and false priorities.[20] Yet God has provided atonement for human sin, deliverance from its deception and bane, and the possibility of a new life in his favor. The good life is marked by the appropriateness of its response to these displays of divine goodness.

2. At several points in his letters, Paul sums up human ethical responsibilities by referring to the duty to love others.[21] Closely related are the charges to his readers to live for the good of others rather than please themselves.[22] A depiction of moral obligation in these terms is, for Paul, merely an alternative way of commending the "appropriate response to God's goodness" mentioned above: those who experience and are transformed by God's goodness respond appropriately with love

19. Philippians 1:27.
20. The preceding summary is based upon Paul's argument in Romans 1:18-32. See Chapter Three above.
21. Romans 13:8-10; Galatians 5:14. Nor should we forget 1 Corinthians 13, his famous hymn to love.
22. Romans 15:1-3; 1 Corinthians 10:24, 33; Galatians 6:2; Philippians 2:4.

for those whom God loves, and with a desire to see God's good purposes realized in their lives.[23] Furthermore, love for others should be possible, even natural, among those freed from anxious self-interest by a trust in God's commitment to their well-being.

For Paul, then, the guiding principle of the good life is the duty to love others. Needless to say, love, for Paul, is not shown in the free expression of emotion but in ways that are informed by, as they represent an appropriate response to, the goodness of God in creation and redemption.

The Good Life

In Romans 12–16, Paul speaks of three contexts in which the "good life" must be lived: in a (non-Christian) society; within the community of believers; and before God.[24] Here we must be content to note briefly the behavior that Paul thinks appropriate in each of these contexts.

1. According to Romans 13:1-7, God has ordained that society be governed by authorities with the power to reward well-doing and to punish evil. Humans prosper when society is stable and the distinction between goodness and evil is recognized and maintained. Concern for human well-being is therefore appropriately shown in respect for such authority and the due payment of taxes and tributes.[25]

Christians are to show their good will toward their neighbors by sharing their good times and bad, "rejoicing with those who rejoice,

---

23. Note Romans 15:1-3, 7; Philippians 2:4-5. The point is clearest in Ephesians 5:2, though the Pauline authorship of the letter is disputed. Cf. also 1 John 4:7-21.

24. A fourth context — that of the family — is not discussed in Romans, though sexual immorality and disobedience to parents are mentioned in Romans 1, where they are seen as expressing humanity's resistance to the goodness of God's created order. See the discussion in Chapters Three and Four above.

25. Paul does not discuss what should be done when rulers fail to promote good and to curb evil, when they maintain their office by show of force rather than by exercising the authority that, according to Paul, accompanies the execution of a divine mandate. We need to remember that Paul was not writing a systematic treatise on life in society, but a letter to a particular community at a particular time. He must have felt that existing circumstances required no more than the broadest statement of principle.

weeping with those who weep."[26] They are to be careful to maintain both a reputation for personal integrity and — to the extent it depends on them — good relations with others.[27] If they are mistreated, they are to determine the tone of their response not by the ill-will of their persecutors but by the good will and love that they have themselves experienced in Christ.[28] Justice should be left in the hands of God, who will ultimately purge his creation of irredeemable evil.[29] The task of God's people is to seek to redeem the evil they encounter by responding in love: to "overcome evil with good."[30] All these instructions follow naturally and appropriately from Paul's vision of reality.

Good relations with others are not, however, to be procured by sharing a lifestyle of loose living, contentiousness, or jealousy. License, self-assertion, and a preoccupation with self-interest are the marks of humanity's rebellion against the divine order of love. They cannot survive the ultimate triumph of the good. Christian behavior is to be aligned unequivocally with the latter.[31]

2. The good life is not lived in isolation, not even in a solitary pursuit of the good. A "worthy" response to God's goodness includes participation in the community of the redeemed.

Within the community, there is to be mutual respect, aid for the needy, hospitality: these are obvious expressions of the Christian duty to love.[32] But most of what Paul says in this context addresses concerns raised by the inevitable diversity of the community of believers. People are not to consider themselves better than others or to keep from associating with them because of an inflated self-image.[33] The community is like a body with different parts, each performing a role important to

26. Romans 12:15.

27. Romans 12:17-18.

28. Romans 12:14, 17.

29. Romans 12:19.

30. Romans 12:21. Romans 12:14, 17-21 provide a close parallel to the words of Jesus in Matthew 5:38-48. "Overcome evil with good" is, in effect, a more prosaic way of saying "Turn the other cheek!" (Matthew 5:39). It seems also to represent Paul's interpretation of the obscure words that close the quotation from Proverbs (25:21-22) given in Romans 12:20: in the light of Romans 12:21, the "coals of fire" experienced by an enemy who is treated with kindness seem to be pangs of remorse that lead to repentance.

31. Romans 13:11-14.

32. Romans 12:9-13.

33. Romans 12:16; note also Romans 12:3.

the functioning of the whole. The ability to carry out a function is itself a gift of God's grace; it demands to be used, as intended, for the good of the whole. Some are to convey messages from God, others to exercise administrative leadership; some to encourage, others to attend in tangible ways to the physical needs of the community. Whatever one's area of service, it must be performed wholeheartedly.[34]

Only one ethical issue is given extended treatment in these chapters: it pertains to diversity within the community of believers and was, presumably, of local concern in Rome.[35] Paul's general discussion of the principles at stake leaves us in doubt about the particulars; but the most likely background, in my judgment, is as follows.

The Christian community in Rome included many non-Jews who had never observed the Mosaic food and festival laws, and perhaps some Jews who had ceased their observance. Both shared Paul's conviction that all foods may be eaten by the one who receives them, with thanks, as gifts from the hand of God. But also within the community were Jewish Christians who kept a more restrictive diet, either because they considered themselves still bound by the laws of Torah or (and Paul's language perhaps favors this second alternative) because a lifetime of observance had left them with scruples that did not disappear when they adopted Christian faith. All were Christians. All intended to express in their eating their devotion to God. But the differences in eating habits threatened to divide the community.

Paul *pre*scribes mutual acceptance, on the principle that those whom God has accepted, his people must be prepared to accept. He *pro*scribes condemning each other on the principle that God is the only competent judge of his servants. He tells those whose conscience forbids them to eat certain foods to follow their convictions. Not that the food itself is inherently "unclean." But everything Christians do is to express their confidence in God's goodness and favor; and no such confidence can be felt by people eating what they sense they ought not to be eating.

Paul's vision of the good determines his response to those with a more robust conscience as well. In principle, he writes, they are free to do what their conscience permits: even the partaking of food, when accompanied by an acknowledgment of their dependence on God, be-

34. Romans 12:3-8.
35. For what follows, see Romans 14:1–15:6.

comes an act of appropriate service. On the other hand, that same act of eating becomes mere self-indulgence if done without consideration of the sensibilities of others. If, by eating, those with a robust conscience cause grief to those more scrupulous than they, or if, by eating, they tempt the more scrupulous to violate their scruples, then the robust have failed in their paramount duty to love. Pleasing God in these cases requires self-sacrifice. The sacrifice is minimal, however, for those whose focus in life is not on food and drink but on right living, peace, and the joy of the presence of God.

Some practices and teachings are directly counter to God's purposes in creation and redemption, expressive rather of self-interest than of service to Christ. Goodwill toward all is not to be confused with naïveté. The believers' mature understanding of the good and of its implications should keep them from being led astray.[36]

3. Those captivated by a sense of God's goodness will want to give themselves to his service. In temples the world over, animals were dedicated to a deity and sacrificed on altars. Paul adopts language from this practice: "Present your bodies as a sacrifice that is living, holy, and pleasing to God; this is your spiritual[37] service."[38] All that Christians do, in society as well as within the community of believers, is to reflect their desire to carry out God's will.[39]

At no point is the difference between Pauline horizons and those of the modern West more apparent. Within the latter, individual freedom and self-fulfillment are for many the highest ideals. For Paul, pleasing oneself is a bad thing, insistence on self-determination is calamitous; conversely, obedience, service, self-sacrifice, even slavery — when God, or the Lord Jesus, is the master — are *positive* terms, the marks of a life worth living.

The differences can be exaggerated, of course, or the point of divergence misconstrued. Moderns, too, know that the furtherance of

36. Romans 16:17-20.

37. The term here almost means "figurative": the metaphorical "sacrifice" of the believer's body is contrasted with the physical sacrificing of animals carried out in temples. At the same time, the Greek word suggests that such dedication to God's service is the "reasonable" path for humans to take.

38. Romans 12:1.

39. Romans 12:2, understood as a statement of principle that encompasses the specific instructions to follow.

a common cause may require some to exercise leadership, others to follow. The modern world, too, witnesses much self-sacrifice that is motivated by love. But obedience and service in these cases are often circumstantial. What the modern world lacks is a vision of reality that would prescribe service as a way of life: a sense that, underlying all, there is goodness both rewarding and worthy of human devotion.

If human existence is an accident, if the functioning of the cosmos is merely mechanical, if the language of right and wrong is rooted in nothing deeper than human convention, if the world is but the indifferent stage on which we give shape to our lives, then we may well resent any attempt to curtail our freedom and self-determination. If, on the other hand, human existence is a gift of love, if the functioning of the cosmos is providential, if language of right and wrong reflects our appropriate and inappropriate responses to reality, and human existence — indeed, all creation — has been cursed by human self-assertion; and if, moreover, Jesus Christ represents God's refusal to abandon his willful creatures to their sin; if Christ demonstrates the goodness of a life lived in obedience to God, his self-sacrificial death atones for human wrongdoing, and his resurrection makes possible eternal life in communion with God as a member of his redeemed people: if all these basic convictions of Paul are true, then (perhaps even moderns would agree) there can be no prouder title than that claimed by the apostle — a "servant of Jesus Christ."[40]

40. Romans 1:1.

Index